THE
SECESSIONIST
STATES OF
AMERICA

THE SECESSIONIST STATES OF AMERICA

THE BLUEPRINT FOR CREATING A TRADITIONAL VALUES COUNTRY...NOW

DOUGLAS MacKINNON

Skyhorse Publishing

Copyright © 2014 by Douglas MacKinnon

The views and opinions expressed here are the author's own and do not necessarily represent the views or opinions of Skyhorse Publishing.

All rights reserved. No part of this book may be reproduced in any manner without the express written consent of the publisher, except in the case of brief excerpts in critical reviews or articles. All inquiries should be addressed to Skyhorse Publishing, 307 West 36th Street, 11th Floor, New York, NY 10018.

Skyhorse Publishing books may be purchased in bulk at special discounts for sales promotion, corporate gifts, fund-raising, or educational purposes. Special editions can also be created to specifications. For details, contact the Special Sales Department, Skyhorse Publishing, 307 West 36th Street, 11th Floor, New York, NY 10018 or info@skyhorsepublishing.com.

Skyhorse® and Skyhorse Publishing® are registered trademarks of Skyhorse Publishing, Inc.®, a Delaware corporation.

Visit our website at www.skyhorsepublishing.com.

10 9 8 7 6 5 4 3 2 1

Library of Congress Cataloging-in-Publication Data is available on file.

Cover design by Richard Rossiter

Print ISBN: 978-1-62914-676-8
Ebook ISBN: 978-1-63220-117-1

Printed in the United States of America

To the tens of millions of Americans who still believe in Traditional Values and who refuse to compromise their beliefs. Patriots all.

"A little rebellion now and then is a good thing...It is a medicine necessary for the sound health of government."
—Thomas Jefferson

"We hold these truths to be self-evident, that all men are created equal, that they are endowed by their Creator with certain unalienable Rights, that among these are Life, Liberty and the pursuit of Happiness.—That to secure these rights, Governments are instituted among Men, deriving their just powers from the consent of the governed, —That whenever any Form of Government becomes destructive of these ends, it is the Right of the People to alter or to abolish it, and to institute new Government, laying its foundation on such principles and organizing its powers in such form, as to them shall seem most likely to effect their Safety and Happiness." —Declaration of Independence, July 4, 1776

"This country, with its institutions, belongs to the people who inhabit it. Whenever they shall grow weary of the existing government, they can exercise their constitutional right of amending it, or their revolutionary right to dismember or overthrow it." —Abraham Lincoln, 1861

"The American Republic will endure until the day Congress discovers that it can bribe the public with the public's money...In a revolution...the most difficult part to invent is the end." —Alexis de Tocqueville

"Those who make peaceful revolution impossible make violent revolution inevitable." —President John F. Kennedy

ACKNOWLEDGMENTS

First and foremost, to Tony Lyons and the staff at Skyhorse Publishing, for your belief in me and this project.

Next, to the men and women behind the scenes who not only brought their expertise to this effort, but who inspired me on a daily basis with their faith, their service, their sacrifice, their certitude, their love of liberty, and their growing belief that a nation built firmly upon the foundation of Traditional Values can once again be a reality. Onward together in a quest to make a positive difference and rebuild that "Shining City Upon A Hill."

TABLE OF CONTENTS

INTRODUCTION

Many times, the "introduction" section of a book gives necessary and sometimes *not so* necessary background on the subject.

Most of the time—at least for the reader in me—like the prologue of a novel, it proves to be an unnecessary false start to what the reader hopes will be an enjoyable and informative experience.

In this case, and in *my* case, I felt a quick, true "introduction" of myself was in order.

It is my sincere hope that this book will be read by as many people as possible. *Obviously.* The main reason I say that is because I want the effort to be worth something. I want it to *mean* something. As you might imagine, many or most will consider the subject matter of this book to be somewhat to very controversial. Some will be comforted by it. Others will be quite alarmed and even threatened by the theme.

Before putting "pen to paper," I gave a great deal of thought to the risks involved in not only writing such a book, but also attaching my name to the project. More than a few people close to me suggested and even *implored* me to use a pseudonym instead of my real name.

I considered the suggestion for about five seconds, then cast it aside.

Because of the controversial nature of this book, I very well may pay a real professional, and even personal, price for writing it. I understand that, but honestly feel my attempt to help jumpstart a serious dialog regarding the options open to those who cherish Traditional Values far outweighs the risk to me or my career.

Another reason I was strongly against using a pseudonym was because I felt my background and real-life experience might mean something to some readers.

Again, I do want as many people as possible to read this book. Everyone from every single demographic across the board will be a valued reader, and I truly believe all can get something out of the effort if they go into the process with an open mind. That said, I wrote this book with *one* particular demographic in mind—that being the hardworking American from every race, creed, and color who tries to play by the rules, who struggles to make ends meet, and who lives his or her life in the most honorable way possible with deference and respect for all.

It is *this* demographic that is the backbone of our country, and it is to that demographic I especially wanted to make something clear: at the very least, this book was not written by some Ivory-Tower academic who has never experienced nor been touched by real life.

For better *and* worse, I have experienced a great deal of real life, and it is my enduring hope that such a background contributes in some way to the foundation of this project.

As you have read in the brief description of me on the jacket, I found some professional success as an adult. But for sure, it was a challenge getting there.

I grew up in abject poverty and was often homeless as a child. By the time I was seventeen years of age, my family had moved thirty-four times. Each move was an eviction; many of them were fairly violent.

In most of those moves, I lived in economically challenged African American or Hispanic American neighborhoods with some of the most impressive adults and children it has ever been my honor to know. At a very early age, I came to the realization that experience meant everything and that, to survive, I had to learn how to understand or adapt to that experience. Nothing to me was "theoretical" or remotely close to the psycho-babble nonsense taught today by those who have learned so little in life.

A few years ago, my memoir was published, the opening words to that book being: "It really does hurt to get stabbed."

My point then and now in mentioning that experience is this: I may know a thing or two about the challenges of life. I do know nothing is easy for most people. I do know of the endless obstacles most have to overcome just to barely provide for themselves and their families. I do know a little something about picking yourself up when knocked into the dirt, dusting yourself off, and starting again with that particular experience now locked into your memory bank as a positive rather than a negative.

No one ever gave me anything in life, and that was okay with me. I wanted to earn my way and honestly relished the challenge. All I asked as a child—and all I continue to ask now—was that neither society nor my own government throw up unnecessary, bureaucratic, or politically correct barriers in my path that would hinder or even crush my effort to carve out a better life.

That, of course, was a hope unrealized for me and for most of us. Those needless barriers *do* exist and they are getting larger and *more* punitive by the day.

* * *

One last point I wanted to make before beginning is that in many ways, this book and this project is *all* about "human dignity" and the "human spirit." This is *not* a partisan issue but rather a *values* issue.

Most people *do* want to stand on their own two feet. Most people *do* want to earn their way in life free of hand-outs and free of entitlements that adversely affect the welfare of others.

For most of us, life *is* hard and life can and *will* be cruel. Knowing that, there is absolutely nothing wrong with charity nor is there anything wrong with asking for a helping hand when needed.

But when we do get charity or we do ask for that helping hand, the question then becomes: Does it motivate us to hopefully never be put in that position again? Or does it instead activate a self-destructive and narcissistic little voice in our head which says, "Hey, having my neighbors do all the work and having my neighbors contribute their hard-earned money to fund my lifestyle of inactivity is a good thing"?

As a child growing up in true poverty, I did learn at any early age that government handouts—while certainly needed from time to time by truly good people facing dire circumstances—were ultimately a deterrent to success masked as charity and only allowed those on the receiving end to exist at best while also creating and enabling an entire class of people to become dependent upon and addicted to government welfare funded entirely by the working people of our country.

Others can and *will* disagree, but based entirely upon *my* real-life experience, I strongly believe that the handouts, restrictions, and draconian dictates of the All-Government Nanny state drastically diminish "human dignity" over time while permanently crushing the "human spirit" if allowed to go on unfettered and unchecked by common sense, individual liberty, faith, and principle.

CHAPTER 1

A NEW VISION FOR AMERICA

How does one begin a discussion regarding the highly controversial subject of a "revolution" within the *United States of America* or "seceding from the Union"?

Well, for me, it began about four years ago at an outdoor café at the Willard Hotel in Washington, DC. I had gone there to meet a longtime friend for "drinks." In his case, a couple of beers. In my case, a couple of Pepsis.

I arrived about 5 p.m. on a July afternoon and my friend was already seated at a table for two fairly isolated from the rest of the patrons enjoying a rare humidity-free day at the height of the summer in our nation's capital.

My friend had served his nation overseas for years as a special operator before retiring and basically doing the same job for a private contractor around the world. Like me—and tens of millions of Americans—he was conservative in nature and a strong believer in Traditional Values.

More than that—also like so many of us—he firmly believed the nation he had sacrificed so much for in voluntary service was disappearing before his eyes and being replaced by an entity at cross-purposes with basically every single thing he believed in, supported, and held dear.

When we met, we had absolutely no agenda in mind. Nothing. The sole purpose of our visit that late afternoon was just to catch up after a few months of not seeing each other and not talking. As the conversation progressed, and after ordering a couple of appetizers, we morphed into a chat about the Republic we both loved coming off the rails and going straight off the bridge into a bottomless abyss.

As we talked, I asked, "So what is your bright solution to this exponentially growing problem?"

He looked up and smiled and answered, "Well, we could always take over another country and recreate the dream of our Founding Fathers within *those* borders."

I laughed. "Oh. Nice to see you picked the simple and easy answer. Have any particular country in mind?"

Without missing a beat, he said, "Australia."

When I asked why Australia, he was equally quick with his response.

"Uncounted natural resources. It's a continent unto itself. It has a relatively small population for its massive land mass, has a number of military bases, has millions of like-minded people—not to mention some of the most stunning women in the world—and other logistics critical to such an operation."

For the next ten minutes or so, he recited those logistics and why they—despite the fact that the incredible and freedom-loving people of Australia might actually *object* to being taken over or marginalized—might work in favor of someone looking to start a new nation.

As a former special operator for our nation, for him, resistance from a native population was just one of the many items on the checklist to be noted and later overcome.

Also, it must be stressed, for *both* of us, this was just an *academic* exercise meant to while away some of our time together.

After drifting from our imaginary conversation about conquering Australia, I asked him a much more serious question:

"What about the United States of America? What about *our* country, *our* soil, *our* people, *our* values, and *our* futures? What, if anything, can be done here?"

BINGO.

We immediately began to kick around a few ideas regarding this also purely "academic" exercise on how one might create a new nation *within* the United States of America built entirely upon the foundation of Traditional Values.

Appetizers soon became dinner, and dinner soon became coffee. At the end of the three-hour catch-up session, we both left the table energized with the thought that maybe we were really onto something. That maybe, at the very least, there was an "academic" ray of hope that could be created and seen by the tens of millions of Americans across the country certain that the nation of their youth and the nation of *their* values was lost forever.

From that dinner, an idea, a dream, this book...and maybe even a better future...were born.

* * *

Days after the dinner, we met again in Washington, DC. Our excitement and energy level hadn't waned with the passing few days—it had grown. Each of us felt we had just planted one tiny seed—arbitrarily or by design—and that the seed, at the very least, was entitled to bit of sunlight and a splash of water.

The major part of that nourishment was to take the very idea and the concerns of tens of millions of Americans seriously. Very seriously.

The best way to do that was to continue the conversation to see where it took us.

We both agreed that the most critical ingredient needed for even an "academic" exercise like ours was experience. *Real-world* experience and lots of it.

If our current president, his team, and their growing list of miscalculations and failures around the country and around the world taught us anything, it's that experience *does* matter. And that a *lack* of that experience has serious, destructive, and lasting consequences.

That said, real-world experience divorced from faith, a moral compass, and certitude could be just as useless and just as dangerous as those "leaders"—like Barack Obama—operating with no relevant experience.

Knowing that, we decided Job One for us was to *expand* our tiny discussion group of two people into a circle of experts from the very walks of life needed—at least on paper—to bring a new nation to life.

Throughout the years, I had the good fortune to meet, stay in contact with, and become friends with an incredibly impressive list of people who more than answered the mail when it came to the expertise needed to explore and expand our subject matter.

On that list was another special operator who spent his career with a three-letter agency, two former ambassadors, two retired high-ranking military officers, a constitutional law expert, a banking expert, an infrastructure expert, an energy expert, two professors, and a farming expert. Others joined the circle on a regular basis.

In person, by phone, or by email, we would communicate regularly and slowly expand upon the initial discussion as we penciled in the roughest of blueprints on Why, How, Where, and even When a new country created in the spirit of Traditional Values would take form.

* * *

As our group continued to expand, we tried to guess how many highly disaffected Americans for whom we might be speaking. Back in 2008, a Zogby International poll found that 22 percent of Americans believed that "any state or region has the right to peaceably secede and become an independent republic."

Okay. That seemed like a reasonable number to us. Twenty-two percent of the population equated to about seventy-two million people.

To be on the ultra-safe side, we then decided to cut that number *in half* and say that at a minimum, approximately thirty-six million Americans were truly disgusted at where the left—and a growing number of "Go along, Get along, Republicans"—was taking our country and would be more than anxious to have ideas, discussion points, and options presented to them in a respectful and realistic manner.

These are Americans, by the way, from every single race, creed, and color. *Every single one.* They are wealthy, they are middle class, and they are poor. Some are desperately poor. Tens of millions of people who are united by a common and unbreakable bond: their belief in Traditional Values and their absolute certainty that those values are no longer represented by their government, their "leaders," and increasingly, not even the clergy of their particular religion. They are positive that no one in authority cares anymore—that most in government, most in the media, most in education, most in entertainment, and even many in business have cast aside ethics, morals, faith, accountability, charity, and even their own survival instinct for the ultra-short-term rewards tied to hedonism, political party, or a failed ideology.

These tens of millions of Americans who *do* believe in Traditional Values feel lost and shunned in their own country.

The number of Americans who believe this is growing every day. Why? A poll by Gallup reported in 2014 alarmingly showed that 72 percent of those polled said, "Big Government is a bigger threat to the future than big business and big labor."

What you are about to read gives those tens of millions of Americans—and maybe even you—a few ideas, discussion points, and options needed to at least start a dialog with others as we all band together in spirit to figure out the best and most viable way to preserve our values and live in peace and prosperity in a Republic that honors them and us.

As a side note entirely pertinent to this subject, "secession" is not just a desire or even movement particular to our country and our set of circumstances; it is part of the "human spirit" when liberty and rights are threatened or trampled. In a poll taken in Canada a few years ago within its four Western provinces, an astounding 36.6 percent of the residents of those provinces said: "Western Canadians should begin to explore the idea of forming their own country."

Freedom-loving and Traditional Values–espousing people any-where—be they in Canada or the United States—should always have the *legal option* open to them to "explore the idea of forming their own country."

Metaphorically, as we turn back to *our* nation and look at con-servatives and liberals—or red states and blue states—as the bride and groom of the marriage that is now the United States of America, then many on both sides of that divide will at least agree on one thing: divorce and the separation of community property is the *only* answer. There is zero hope of reconciliation, and being forced every day to be together in exponentially growing misery and anger not only damages this ideological couple, but also inflicts perma-nent harm upon the institution of that marriage as symbolized by the United States of America.

At least thirty million of us think that, in the defense of our values, the steam valve must be opened and a new institution must be created.

* * *

That's one basic and simplified example. Now let's get back to the *reality* of the situation and the *message* of this book. What you are about to read and digest and use as a discussion tool is also going to make others from the left—or even the entrenched establishment of the Republican Party—more than a little nervous and then quite vocal.

Why?

"Our" government has dangerously assumed too much power and the people who either gave it that power, benefit from that power, abuse that power, or simply have gotten used to getting something for nothing *because* of that power want to keep it that way. At any cost.

Ironically, in May of 2014, James Comey, the director of the FBI appointed by Barack Obama, spoke to this issue of government power at a hearing before Congress. Said the FBI director in part:

> I believe people should be suspicious of government power. I am. I think this country was founded by people who were worried about government power so they divided it among three branches.

How correct the director of the FBI is to make that assessment. But what if—as more and more Americans are coming to believe—all three branches of our federal government are derelict in their duties and collectively abusing their "divided" power? What then?

Hence, this book.

* * *

As I write this book, we still have the First Amendment—which guarantees free speech. I will assume—and that's a *very* risky assumption of late—that the First Amendment will still exist upon publication of this book. If so, then those inclined to attack the premise of this book or to attack me, or both, as "radical," "treasonous," "dangerous," or "fostering revolution" need to do several things, the first of which being to calm down and realize that we do have free speech in this country, as much as some on the left—or the establishment—would like to shut it down.

The second thing they need to do is read and absorb the words of Thomas Jefferson, Abraham Lincoln, and others who did strongly believe that free people should always be presented with a set of options when their liberty and values are threatened or taken from them.

Last, before the ignorant critics or haters try to censor the book or shout me down, they may actually want to *read* the book to learn what is inside its pages. The left often goes after conservatives and Christians as "ignorant book burners," but I have no doubt that many liberals, many members of the mainstream media, and more than a few politicians will be taking a Bic lighter to this book without having read one word other than the title.

That is their right.

But...should they instead take the time to actually *read* the book in its entirety before denouncing it or me, they *will* learn something and then discover there is absolutely nothing "radical," "treasonous," or "dangerous" in this book. They will discover that it simply amplifies the words and ideas of some of our most revered presidents, Founding Fathers, and leaders.

After all, what is wrong or illegal with wanting, hoping, and dreaming of living in a country that puts the rights of the individual before the rights of the state? What is wrong or illegal with wanting, hoping, and dreaming of living in a country that respects Traditional Values? What is wrong or illegal with wanting, hoping, and dreaming of living in a nation that respects liberty?

And finally, what is wrong or illegal about putting out a book with the express purpose of creating a serious dialog aimed at elevating the issue in a way that gives tens of millions of people hope that their concerns and their fears are valid and need to be addressed.

The last time I checked, that was "The American Way." That said, all that I held or hold dear about our Republic, including at least my definition of "The American Way," is deteriorating rapidly and permanently.

Reflecting upon the words of Jefferson, Lincoln, and de Tocqueville that open this book, a few things now become clearer with each passing day:

It *has* become "necessary for one people to dissolve the political bands which have connected them with another." This country *does* "belong to the people who inhabit it," and tens of millions of those people *have* "grown weary of the existing government" for, among other reasons, Congress *has* discovered "that it can bribe the public with the public's money."

And to de Tocqueville's most critical point that "[i]n a revolution, as in a novel, the most difficult part is to invent the end," it must now be noted that the end *has* been invented by a dedicated group of patriots and *will* be offered up in the pages of this book as one possible solution to our "irreconcilable differences."

* * *

The question of our time, the question of our lives is: Do we dare to dream of such a quest?

If we believe in Traditional Values, how can we not? If we believe in *liberty*, how can we not? If we want *better lives* for those who come after us, how can we not?

As a young boy, I saw the play *Man of La Mancha* and first learned of the "impossible" glorious quest of Don Quixote. From that multi award–winning play came "The Impossible Dream"— one of the most inspirational and moving songs of all time. A song that speaks to honor. A song that speaks to sacrifice. A song that speaks to character. A song that speaks to faith. A song that speaks to all who believe in Traditional Values and who cherish liberty.

Below are the relevant lyrics to that song that speaks to this cause:

To dream...the impossible dream...
To fight...the unbeatable foe...
To run...where the brave dare not go...
No matter how hopeless, no matter how far...
To fight for the right, without question or pause...
To be willing to march into Hell for a Heavenly cause...

Is living in a nation built upon the foundation of Traditional Values hopeless? Are the totalitarian dictates of the ALL-Government—my definition of the Nanny state on steroids—and socialism an "unbeatable foe"? Is a better and more prosperous and secure life for those who come after us the "unreachable star"?

For most, it appears that way for the moment.

But for me, I am convinced beyond a shadow of doubt that there are tens of millions of Americans "willing to march into hell for a heavenly cause."

Tens of millions of people are ready, willing, and more than able to embark on "a glorious quest."

* * *

There is nothing remotely "radical" about the people who might want to embark on that *glorious quest* to inhabit such a country. All the opposite.

They are normal men and woman who feel terribly disconnected to what used to be the United States of America while also experiencing a powerful urge to be part of something larger than themselves, larger than their individual problems.

They *are* willing to follow.

But to take such an uncertain and historic step, they need *real* leadership. They need direction. They need certitude. More than anything, they need to know they are not alone in this quest and this is a movement that will not be abandoned by the frivolous or weak.

These thirty or so million Americans *are* prepared—in one way or another—to fight for these rights. But to do so, they need to also be inspired by a realistic blueprint crafted by those who bring conviction, experience, ideas, and most of all *hope* to the table.

As these freedom-loving Americans watch the country they love erode before their eyes, hope becomes *everything*. Without hope, there is nothing.

Thanks in large measure to the team behind this project, there *will* be hope.

The team helping to support this project understands that the hopes and dreams of these thirty million or so Americans now rest, to some extent, in their strong, calm, and experienced hands. They take that cherished responsibility *very* seriously. So seriously, in fact, that they felt it was *their* responsibility to involve themselves in this project.

With that involvement came their further responsibility to give their very best. Part of that "very best" was to draft an honest and realistic blueprint intended to jumpstart a meaningful dialog in the nation.

At least as far as that requirement is concerned, the men and women of this "S" (for "secession") Team feel they have fulfilled their initial obligation and drafted such a plan: a plan of promise, a plan of inspiration.

But mostly, a plan of *hope*—the kind of hope that seeks to reassure Americans who believe in Traditional Values that they *don't* have to surrender. They *don't* have to capitulate. They *don't* have to accept the dictates of the All-Government Nanny state. They *can* fight back. They *can* resist. They *can* win by following the advice of Jefferson and Lincoln.

So . . . the time is now. The stage is set. The players are gathering.

With all that in mind, I am reminded of the age-old dilemma for those who seek to bring about positive change: "If not us, *who*? If not now, *when*?"

* * *

On a closing note to this section, it's important to stress that I have been around the block a few times in life, that I did spend a number of years working for the government of the United States of America, and that a healthy dose of caution and even paranoia can prove to be warranted and even protective from time to time.

Precisely because I am not naïve nor inexperienced, as stressed earlier, I do fully understand that with the writing and publication of this book I—along with the men and women advising this project—am assuming some degree of risk. Be that risk personal, professional, or something a bit more intriguing, it's something we all agreed was our responsibility to take.

As I am now adding the finishing touches to the manuscript, it is March 2014. With just that hint of paranoia bouncing around in my mind, I can report that my desktop computer, my laptop, and my iPhone have now all been hacked—very professionally and all at the same time.

I am all for being very open to innocent or logical explanations, but three different devices all in my name getting hit at the same time is stretching anyone's odds of it just being purely coincidental.

Another one of my friends was also a special operator for our nation and has lent his considerable experience to this project. More than that, having now successfully transitioned to private life, he works with a team of six similarly experienced experts. After telling my friend what happened to my devices, and after more discussion and investigation, we determined that there was no doubt a hacking took place.

"What's the big deal?" I said to him. "There are a number of individuals and groups around the nation who have at least openly discussed seceding from their state of even the Union."

My special operator friend had a quick and very convincing answer to that.

"First of all," he said. "I can assure you that *all* of those people have been or are being monitored depending upon their level of expertise, contacts, and capability. Second, because *you* have worked in the White House, the Pentagon, and with other agencies within our government, you would be automatically elevated to a much higher level of interest. Your government background combined with *your extensive media platform* would certainly pique not only the curiosity of those from *our* government tasked with monitoring such issues and people, but the curiosity of those from certain foreign governments tasked with that surveillance as well. Now, as the cat was officially let out of the bag in January of 2014 and this concentrated hacking started soon thereafter, it's safe to assume that two plus two does equal four in this case."

What my friend was referring to when he talked about "the cat being out of the bag" was the fact that my incredibly professional and courageous publisher—Skyhorse Publishing—listed the book for pre-sale on Amazon and some other online bookseller sites in January 2014. Prior to that, of course, the title and parts of the manuscript were making some of the usual rounds in the publishing world and were known to a handful of people.

As much of the American public and the media are coming to learn from the cascading number of "NSA Spying Stories," our government—as well as other powerful nations like Russia and China—has very sophisticated computer software programs that search out keywords. If the software finds such keywords, a red flag is triggered and some degree of activity commences.

Would the title of this book, *The Secessionist States of America: A Blueprint for Creating a Traditional Values Country . . . Now,* trigger such a red flag? Be those red flags in Washington, DC, Moscow, or Beijing?

Only the software and the analysts monitoring it can say for sure, but it's a very safe assumption that the title and its stated objective would create *some* activity in those arenas.

That said, *long before* "the cat was out of the bag," I had made the decision to write the manuscript and keep all my notes and contacts associated with the project on a separate computer that has *never been online and has never been on the Grid.*

Of course, being deliberately cautious in this case also seems prudent if we stop to realize that *as you are reading this,* the

Department of Homeland Security and FEMA are conducting aggressive Cyber Operations against numerous libertarian, Christian, or conservative groups they have labeled as "Extremist Right-Wing Radicals."

As we have also learned, "our" government respects the privacy of *no one* and considers any and all Americans and American groups a potential threat. The hacking into the computers of the United States Congress, where entire files were suddenly and very mysteriously read, copied, altered, or deleted altogether, is a chilling example that no one is exempt from such surveillance.

Understanding that new and very permanent reality of life, to protect the book and the very intent of this project, I also started to inform as many people as possible within the conservative and Traditional Values media of the contents of the manuscript and when it would be published.

As continually stated and reemphasized, this project—should it come to fruition—would only be done in a legal, peaceful, and constitutional manner. That said, the very mention of the topic of *secession* by someone with my multiple high-level contacts from the government, the private sector, and the conservative media does understandably make some people in Washington nervous and some intelligence operatives from others nations curious.

I—and the team helping behind the scenes—get that. Hence, everything was created and stored offline and off the Grid.

Hopefully, with this book and its mission now being an "Open Secret" and known to millions, anyone who was tracking the project will now move on to other targets.

Ironically, we are just exercising our rights as American citizens. Anything wrong with *that?*

CHAPTER 2

REVOLUTION IS PART OF OUR HISTORY AND IS IN OUR BLOOD

The exponentially growing chaos of the day serves as a stark and tragic reminder that the status quo is not working and brings to mind the warning from Albert Einstein who wisely observed that the definition of *insanity* is doing the same thing over and over again and expecting different results.

Our nation and the world is doing the same thing over and over again and...creating the *exact* same tragic results.

Knowing that, the question then becomes: How do you—how do *we*—change the equation? *How* do we change the dynamic? How do we get the country and the world to stop the insanity of purposely replicating the same mistakes over and over again that then have a negative—and many times catastrophic—impact upon most of us?

One possible way—and the solution offered up in the pages of this book—is to finally take control of our own destiny by making and then living by our own rules.

One way to do this, as spelled out by Thomas Jefferson and Abraham Lincoln, is to legally, peacefully, and constitutionally create our own nation where we could, once and for all, stop the insanity of those destined to destroy themselves and take us down with them in the process.

As this "insanity" plays out, there are always tipping points that force the scale to crash to one side or the other. For the tens of millions of Americans from every walk of life who do believe in and cherish Traditional Values, the *left* side of that scale has now loudly, completely, and permanently crashed to the ground from the exponentially growing weight of the All-Government Nanny state programs heaped upon it by the (mostly very wealthy) far-left activists in politics, the media, academia, entertainment, and even Wall Street who deem to decide the fate for the rest of us—liberal activists, by the way, who *never* expect to exist under the politically correct rules, laws, programs, or individualist-crushing constraints they continually impose upon those Americans who have less wealth and "social status" than them.

As this destructive reality continues unabated, it should be known by those on both sides of the political spectrum and within the mainstream media, that the only true motivation behind this movement *is* peaceful, legal, and constitutional.

For myself and the advisors behind the scenes, that is the only way we *could* operate for the simple and pure reason that we love, at least, the *concept* of what our country *used* to be and respect and believe in the Constitution and the Declaration of Independence.

As such, there truly is a method behind the "madness," a process that has been carefully thought out by our team. And one—which for those "academic" purposes of course—could be launched when and if the proper people and logistics were in place.

That said, this type of ambitious and highly controversial premise *is* a process. An incredibly complicated emotional, patriotic, and logistical process, but still . . . a process.

Steps must be followed. Laws must be obeyed. The current government of the United States of America—as broken as most of us believe it to be—*must* be respected. And above all, the American people—liberal, conservative, libertarian, or agnostic of government beliefs—*must* be honored.

This process, this movement, this *quest* for a life built upon and supported by the pillars of Traditional Values *will* honor the people. It and we could do no less.

Knowing all that to be true, we are faced with the question: Are we about to reach that *final* tipping point here in the United States of America of today?

As we ponder that question—with most of us already knowing the answer—it would be instructive to look at a few of the most famous and infamous tipping points of our earliest history as well as the first two American Revolutions as we analyze what may constitute the "final" tipping point for the *third* American Revolution.

* * *

THE PILGRIMS COME TO THE NEW WORLD

On September 6, 1620, the Pilgrims—or the "Religious Radicals" as the left-of-center History Channel calls them—set sail on a sixty-five-day treacherous journey across the Atlantic Ocean in search of religious freedom.

At this point, I'd like to pause to make an editorial comment—something I will do from time to time but always promise to be on topic with the comments.

As the book progresses, I will outline more of the legitimate reasons why tens of millions of Americans feel abandoned by not only their "government" and "leaders," but also by what passes for news, entertainment, and education.

More than abandoned, when it comes to the media, many times Americans of faith and Traditional Values feel constantly marginalized, vilified, ostracized, and...betrayed.

The "History" Channel with its liberal and far-left agenda is just one of the sources of this continual attack on the beliefs and faith of Americans who do believe in Traditional Values.

If we put the History Channel aside for a moment and tune in to other cable outlets such as the Science Channel, we will find a *cottage industry* of programming all filmed and aired with one purpose in mind: to *prove* that God does not exist.

Really? The left and these liberal "scientists" have nothing better to do with their time, and often *our* tax dollars, than to spend their waking hours seeking to disprove the existence of God?

As many of these far-left scientists and cable network executives clearly came to believe that Barack Obama *was* and *is* the Messiah, then doesn't their unshakeable belief in Mr. Obama and their many words and deeds elevating him to this deity status mean they failed in their own pointless quest? With that belief in Mr. Obama, didn't these scientists expose themselves as "academic" frauds?

While Barack Obama became a deity to many on the left, one can at least guess that the *real* God the vast majority of Americans believe in and know to be real may take a dim view of these "scientists," cable executives, professors, reporters, and actors spending so much time and effort trying to disprove Him.

With the exponentially growing misery in the world—much of it created or enabled by socialist, Marxist, and politically correct dictates—one could also at least guess that the real God most of us believe in and know to be real might wish these non-believers and lost souls would instead concentrate their considerable collective talents and resources toward curing diseases and helping the less fortunate.

Tragically and quite selfishly, they don't.

While He may wish them to experience a change of heart, we know that is likely never going to happen, as many on the far-left seem consumed by their hate of Christianity or faith in general.

This is bizarre, troubling, and quite dangerous, to say the least.

* * *

Okay, now back to those "Religious Radicals," as labeled by the History Channel.

The Pilgrims were, in fact, in search of religious freedom. Again, this is something many of us today can understand as we witness certain faiths and certain believers under constant attack— be those attacks openly bigoted and discriminatory in nature as in the United States or murderous and genocidal in nature as we are witnessing in other parts of the world. (An escalation of murder and genocide is being carried out against Christians and Jews and has been all but ignored by the mainstream media here in the United States, Canada, and Europe.) History does indeed repeat itself and always will unless people of good will and faith rise up against evil.

So, on September 6, 1620, 102 passengers boarded the Mayflower with most hoping and praying to find that religious freedom in the New World. For their beliefs and for their liberty, they were willing to risk their very lives so that they may live in peace.

Far from the "Radicals" as painted by the History Channel, these were men and women looking simply to make a break from the Anglican Church of England. As Separatist Protestants, they believed in strict adherence to the Word of Jesus Christ as taken directly from the New Testament of the Bible.

Two days after making landfall in the New World, the Pilgrims wrote and ratified what became known as the Mayflower Compact.

Part of that compact read:

Having undertaken for the Glory of God, and Advancement of the Christian Faith, and the honor of our King and Country, a voyage to plant the first colony in the northern parts of Virginia; do these presents, solemnly and mutually in the Presence of God and one another, covenant and combine ourselves together into a civil Body Politick, for our better Ordering and Preservation, and Furtherance of the Ends aforesaid.

"Radical" only to someone from the far-left trying to squash *certain* religions and silence *certain* believers.

* * *

Speaking of those Pilgrims, Fox News personality and libertarian John Stossel authored a column for FoxNews.com that dramatically outlined why socialism will always fail when and if it competes with free market capitalism and plain old-fashioned hard work.

As Mr. Stossel related: "Had today's political class been in power in 1623, then 'Thanksgiving' would have been called 'Starvation Day.'"

Mr. Stossel, who has long annoyed the far-left and their political, academic, and media enablers by exposing their agenda, lies, or both, then went on to accurately explain and defend his opinion. Mr. Stossel said in part:

---

from "The Lost Lesson of Thanksgiving," FoxNews.com, November 2010

Long before the failure of modern socialism…the Pilgrims at Plymouth Colony organized their farm economy along communal lines. The goal was to share the work and produce equally.

That's why they nearly all starved.

When people can get the same return with less effort, most people make less effort. Plymouth settlers faked illness rather than working the common property. Some even stole, despite their Puritan convictions…

Mr. Stossel went on to relate that Governor William Bradford and the leadership of the Pilgrims quickly realized the error of their ways and switched from Socialism to Capitalism and because of that change *lived* to celebrate the first Thanksgiving in November of 1623.

Try to find *that* lesson in the politically correct "history" books in our public and private schools of today.

* * *

THE *FIRST* AMERICAN REVOLUTION

THE REVOLUTIONARY WAR

As like *now*, there were a number of issues throughout a number of years and decades that finally coalesced into the tipping points that galvanized our Founding Fathers and the citizens of pre–Revolutionary War America to act.

Before going into that, I would like to offer up another editorial comment that goes directly to yet *another* reason tens of millions of Americans who do believe in Traditional Values are frustrated beyond belief.

That editorial comment is the fact that liberal America—and again, by that I mean the wealthy liberal activists who control most of our political and judicial system and almost all the media, academia, and "entertainment,"—no longer *allows* anyone to utter the words *Founding Fathers*. Ever. Period.

These All-Government activists—including President Obama (or former president Obama, depending upon when you are reading this book)—*only* refer to the Founding Fathers as "The Founders."

For liberals, it's a crime against political correctness to admit that The Founders were actually all men. Because of their twisted way of thinking, if they refer to the men who brought forth our new nation as the "Founding Fathers," that is somehow an insult to women.

As we know, for many liberals, it's not enough to *not* acknowledge the truth of history; many times those who have the power literally try to *change* history to make it fit neatly and dishonestly into the prism of liberal thought.

* * *

Okay, with that particular editorial comment addressed, back to some of the tipping points for the American Revolutionary War. At least, those not revised and updated later by liberal "historians" or liberal Hollywood.

Very much like now, in the mid-1700s, a number of American Colonists become more and more frustrated with, and alarmed by, excessive taxes imposed upon them by the British Crown as well as the fact that they felt their rights as citizens were being violated in a consistent and growing manner by over-government regulation and needless interference of free enterprise and civil liberties.

One of the earliest tipping points that greatly concerned the Colonists and motivated them to defy the Crown was The Molasses Act of 1733.

This dictate, passed and vigorously pushed by the British Parliament, was meant as a way to force the Colonists into buying higher-priced British molasses. At that time, molasses was one of the key drivers of the Colonial economy. Knowing that, the British Crown imposed very high and punitive taxes upon imported French molasses to force the hand of the Colonists by leaving them only one real option.

Instead, the plan backfired as a number of Colonists went into the smuggling business out of an acute sense of self-preservation. Beyond that, as they went about avoiding British soldiers and tax collectors while creating a thriving shadow economy, they realized they did not *need* the British Empire—with its excessive taxes and nonstop governmental interference—to survive.

In a very real sense, this is when the light bulb went on and the first real stirrings of independence started to take root.

One of the next tipping points of note for the Colonists was the Proclamation of 1763.

On paper, at least, the proclamation was a way for the British Crown to try and foster peace in the colonies after the conclusion of the French and Indian War. They did this by drawing a line down the western boundaries of the Colonies, ostensibly saying all the Colonists had to stay east of the line, with everything west reserved for the Native American Indian population.

Many of the Colonists soon realized there was also an ulterior motive behind this act of "kindness" by the British Crown; the act served as yet another way to control and tax the Colonists. More than that, the Colonists were angered by the fact that the British Crown was impeding their rights as individuals as well and greatly weakening their ability to provide for themselves and their families by forcing them to live and work in one region while ordering them not to settle in areas rich in natural resources and, thus, depriving them of a much better future.

By this point, the fuse of revolution had been lit and was starting to burn brightly.

The very next year came The Sugar Act.

After the French and Indian War, the British Crown found itself deeply in debt. What better way to raise money than to impose yet *another* tax on the Colonists? And so it did with The Sugar Act of 1764. This particular tax had a debilitating effect on the Colonial economy of the time. Worse than that were the draconian steps the British Crown took to enforce the collection of their newest tax. Among those steps was the creation of Admiralty Courts where the Colonists were tried (and almost always convicted) without a jury.

That very same year came The Currency Act. Through this act, the British Crown was able to nationalize and assume complete control of the banking system of the Colonies. With each passing day, the Colonists realized that more independence was being taken away from them by an increasingly greedy government thirsty for power, complete control, complete obedience, and a never-ending tax stream that flowed directly into the pockets of the British Crown. (Again, this is a reality in 1764 that rings even truer in 2014 and beyond.)

Three more tipping points helped to foster one of the most infamous events to occur in the pre-revolutionary Colonies: The Stamp Act of 1765, The Quartering Act of 1765, and The Townshend Acts of 1767 and 1768.

The Stamp Act placed *yet another* tax on the Colonists. This time, a tax was placed on virtually any paper good ever used in the colonies. This particular tax proved to be highly punitive to the Colonists for the obvious reasons. Next came The Quartering Act, which forced the Colonists to house, feed, and buy supplies for British soldiers. Again, this was yet another way for the British Crown to control the Colonists while forcing them to pay tax after tax without representation. After that came The Townshend Acts, which instituted yet another new series of taxes upon the Colonists.

By now, the nerves of the Colonists were on razor edge more than they ever had been. Tensions were about to boil over.

And boil over they did on March 10, 1770, when a Boston teenager was assaulted by a British soldier. Angered by this attack on an unarmed boy, Bostonians gathered in protest to make their feelings known to the soldier. The British Army soon called in reinforcements. Tragically, those reinforcements fired upon the unarmed citizens. After the shooting stopped, eleven Bostonians lay dead or wounded in the street.

Paul Revere and Samuel Adams were then tasked with spreading the word near and far of this armed attack by the British Crown against unarmed civilians, an attack that became known as the Boston Massacre.

This was a crime perpetrated against innocent civilians who had simply reached their breaking point after years and years of exponentially growing abuse by the British Crown—abuse that manifested in endless taxes heaped upon the Colonists coupled with more of their liberty being stripped from them for the greater glory of the British Crown and its all-consuming Big Government appetite.

(Once again . . . sound familiar?)

* * *

In a very real sense, the revolution of 1776 goes on to this day. Only today, it can be argued that we are in *worse* shape with regard to preserving liberty and our overall security—*much* worse shape.

Then, it was about, among other things, taxation without representation and the growing infringement upon our very liberty by the British Sovereign. Today, it involves our greater loss of liberty—be it government infringement on religious liberty, the sanctity of marriage between a man and a woman, over-taxation, the financial collapse of our cities, counties, and states due to the entitlement mentality, and more specifically, the trillions (that's Trillions with a "T") in unfunded public employee pensions, the nonstop attacks upon Traditional Values and their continual erosion, our unsecured borders, no domestic or foreign policy plans to speak of, and the constant assault on the morals of our children by the "entertainment" industry.

No matter where they turn, those who cherish Traditional Values see nothing but a wasteland filled with obstacles intended to impede or suspend their very liberty.

THE *SECOND* AMERICAN REVOLUTION
THE AMERICAN CIVIL WAR

Today, in what passes for the teaching of American History in most of our schools, the American Civil War is given little or no attention. And what attention it does receive is problematic on a number of levels.

Most middle and high schools—and for that matter, most US colleges and universities—teach that the American Civil War was fought over slavery.

That is only *part* of the very complicated and tragic rationale.

"States Rights" in fact played a large role in the reason eleven southern states seceded from the Union to form the Confederate States of America.

As for slavery, it was obscene in its concept, inhumane in its practice, and serves as the most shameful era in our history. Ironically, in spite of the fact that a number of our Founding Fathers were slave owners (or at least ambivalent about the subject), the Declaration of Independence still managed to quite forcefully and eloquently articulate why the owning of one human being by another was and will always remain a crime against humanity.

Said the Declaration:

We hold these truths to be self-evident, that all men are created equal, that they are endowed by their Creator with certain unalienable Rights, that among these are Life, Liberty and the pursuit of Happiness.

As our Founding Fathers were human and therefore flawed and imperfect—as demonstrated by the beliefs of some with regard to slavery—we can forgive them for saying that "All *men* are created equal..."

While Thomas Jefferson is often given the credit for writing the Declaration of Independence, it was in fact drafted by a committee of five men appointed by the Continental Congress: Jefferson, Benjamin Franklin, John Adams, Robert Livingston, and Roger Sherman.

Now, while we all agree it is not wise nor ethical to *revise* history, few would argue that, had this committee of true Patriots drafted the Declaration of Independence today, they would have substituted the word *humans* for *men*.

As we are *all* God's children, there can be no doubt that "all *humans* are created equal." So, for those men and women of true faith around the world, slavery represents a true sin against the will of God. If you are agnostic or an atheist, then it is simply a crime against humanity.

Even though slavery was and always will be truly evil, it still *was* a fact of life in the United States of America of 1860 and a very complicated issue to resolve, especially if you happened to be from the South.

Many times, of course, what does pass for "history" lessons—often being taught in our public schools by teachers with biased agendas—work overtime to vilify the South and demonize *all*—at least the white males—who lived in those states at the time of the American Civil War.

The fact is, *many* people in the southern states also believed slavery to be an abomination of the first order. That said, slavery had also come to serve as an integral part of the southern economy and to abolish it meant inflicting great economic hardship across the much less industrialized South.

Of course, the vilification process of the "Confederate South" goes on to this day. Most on the left and a number of people on the right will tell you that the *Confederate flag* is a "symbol of hate" and its very image must be permanently eradicated from our nation.

But should it be? Was it a "symbol of hate" for the southern states that flew it during the American Civil War? Was it a "symbol of hate" for hundreds of thousands of young men who served and died in its shadow during the American Civil War? Hundreds of thousands of *Americans*.

It must be remembered that to this very day, no war has claimed more American lives than our own Civil War. Upwards of 750,000 men from the North and South were killed, with more than 300,000 of those casualties coming from the South.

Just to try and put those horrific numbers into some kind of perspective, the entire population of the United States during the Civil War was approximately thirty-one million people—less than one-tenth of what it is now.

Civil War deaths of 750,000 represented about 2.5 percent of the population.

To translate that number into today's population would mean that if the exact same percentage were lost in a Civil War in the United States of now, it would equate to more than eight million Americans killed—a truly incomprehensible number to most of us.

During that time of unimagined loss, the Confederate States of America lost today's equivalent of more than three million young men.

While our history courses of today never teach it, the fact of the matter is that, as mentioned, the vast majority of those young men were not fighting and dying to preserve slavery. *Far from it.* Most of them had no connection to slavery and most did not give it a thought one way or another.

Like the tens of millions of young men who have lost their lives in battle through the ages, for the most part, those who fought for the Confederate States of America were either fighting because they were conscripted into battle or because they were simply trying to protect their homes, their families, and their towns. The "politics" of the war was way above their pay grade.

Again, many of the young men who fought and died under the "Stars and Bars" found slavery reprehensible. To these innocent young men, the Confederate flag was not a "symbol of hate," but rather the banner they followed into battle to protect their homes and families.

That is understood and undeniable reality. Why let the *facts* get in the way of wiping forever from our history the flag that flew over the hundreds of thousands of young men who died for the Confederate States of America?

How easy it is for many today to label that flag a "symbol of hate."

Maybe, just maybe, we might want to debate the subject a bit more and look at it from the perspective of these mostly innocent young men lost in battle as opposed to through the politically correct lens of today.

Like it or not, that flag *was part* of our history and *should remain* part of our history.

* * *

As pointed out earlier, with regard to the Confederate Flag or a host of issues, many liberals or those from the far-left of the political spectrum try, often successfully, to bend history to fit their views of how life *should* have been under liberal dictate.

Well-known filmmaker Steven Spielberg, for example, is not only one of the most powerful people in Hollywood, but he, like his business partner Jeffrey Katzenberg, is one of the most generous supporters of liberal and Democrat candidates and causes.

Nothing at all wrong with that. As most conservatives would agree, it is Mr. Spielberg's hard-earned money and he has the right to spend it any way he wants in a lawful manner free from government interference or censorship.

Beyond that, most conservatives would agree—despite his liberal activism—that he is an exceptional filmmaker and storyteller.

But those gifts of Mr. Spielberg's—as acclaimed, as real, and as incredible as they truly are—can also be used for unethical propaganda purposes intended solely to advance a highly flawed and destructive liberal agenda by painting "history" as how he and other liberals would like it to have been as opposed to how it really was.

As mentioned, one quick and continual way to do that is to *always* refer to the Founding Fathers as The Founders. Cheap, easy, and sadly effective.

Another much more effective and insidious way to do it would be to make a major film and purposefully change the "history" of the time to reflect the far-left's political views of today. One such film was Mr. Spielberg's Academy Award–winning movie *Lincoln*.

Just so everyone understands the full context of this liberal manipulation of history, Spielberg's movie was based, in part, on far-left "historian" Doris Kearns Goodwin's book, *Team of Rivals: The Political Genius of Abraham Lincoln*.

As another unfortunate side note of which many of those who believe in Traditional Values are all too aware, basically *all* "historians" we see on national television or who are quoted in the mainstream media are themselves far-left propagandists striving to push a socialist agenda while vilifying those who don't agree with their ideology.

These "historians" have come to represent the pinnacle of the liberal *thought-police*.

For the writing of this "biographical" film, Mr. Spielberg mostly relied on a gentleman by the name of Tony Kushner. For his part, Mr. Kushner proclaimed that Abraham Lincoln's "abolitionist ideals" made him appealing to a Jewish writer and that, although Abraham Lincoln was a *Christian*, he noted the president rarely quoted the New Testament and that his "thinking and his ethical deliberation seem very Talmudic."

Okay. Certainly an interesting and noteworthy interpretation by this liberal screenwriter. As Mr. Kushner believes Abraham Lincoln to be "the greatest Democratic Leader in the World," I wonder what he would make of Mr. Lincoln's quote that appears at the beginning of this book.

No matter what he thinks, it's safe to assume that Mr. Kushner, like Mr. Spielberg, views the world—also from his own wealthy Ivory Tower—through a liberal and false lens.

As such, the actual history of the time had to be altered to reflect this liberal utopia as seen by the likes of Mr. Kushner and Mr. Spielberg.

Like some of the greatest and most destructive propagandists of the mid-twentieth century, Mr. Spielberg and his like-minded collection of sycophants knew the most effective way to spread their alternative view of history was to attempt to fool as many people as possible into believing their revisionist writing.

Ironically again, the man who liberal screenwriter Mr. Kushner called "the greatest Democratic Leader in the World" also had a strong opinion regarding the deliberate attempts to deceive the American people. Said our sixteenth president with regard to this subject:

> You can fool some of the people all of the time, and all of the
> people some of the time, but you cannot fool all of the people all
> of the time.

How truly disgraceful then, that approximately 150 years later, Mr. Kushner uses the most historic and sacred moments in the life of Abraham Lincoln to attempt to "fool some of the people all of the time" by inserting politically correct nonsense into the film.

What nonsense might that be? While there is a great deal of revisionist nonsense to highlight, one reviewer from *The Jewish Daily Forward* summed up much of the problem quite nicely:

from **"Spielberg's Portrait of Lincoln Is A Bust,"** *The Jewish Daily Forward*, **November 2012**

My suspicion that Steven Spielberg can't really do historical films isn't anything new... Maybe this is because narrative clarity and fluidity always count for more with Spielberg than historical precision...I think that part of what keeps *Lincoln* so far away from any mythical past I can believe in is a form of political correctness that often resembles petrification. It's so hot and bothered about getting things wrong that it can't find many ways of getting things right. For starters, most of the black characters in this story—including the private and corporal Union soldiers, both apparently fictional, who are shown in the first scene meeting Lincoln and then proudly quoting him—are plainly 20th-century figures in speech and body language, not inhabitants of the 19th century...

Still on the subject of revisionist history, another writer from the far-left publication *Slate* unintentionally exposed his bias against the truth when writing about *Lincoln*'s highly fictionalized wife Mary Todd Lincoln as played by Sally Field:

from **"Was Mary Todd Lincoln Really 'Insane'?,"** **Slate.com, November 2012**

In one of the movie's best moments, Mrs. Lincoln drolly spars with Thaddeus Stevens (Tommy Lee Jones)

> while her husband looks on in mild terror, capably lacerating him even to his own apparent amusement. Call the scene revisionist, but it reflects the satisfying complexity Spielberg and Kushner see in Mrs. Lincoln...

"Call the scene revisionist..." says the liberal writer. Are you kidding me? It *is* revisionist. It's all made to push the agenda of the filmmakers. As is a much more ridiculous scene at the end of the movie where the camera pans back from Thaddeus Stevens in bed (again, played by Al Gore's roommate from college Tommy Lee Jones) and we see him sleeping with his African American housekeeper. Political correctness and the world *as it should have been* brought to you by Spielberg and Kushner.

Again, this is not filmmaking but rather a deliberate attempt to revise history while fooling as many people as possible. And guess what? It is working.

Sadly, most Americans are not aware of the facts surrounding the Civil War, President Lincoln's true beliefs, or the passage of the Thirteenth Amendment. As such, many walked out of the movie *Lincoln* believing much or all of the politically correct reinvention of history to be pure fact. The shame for that starts with the filmmakers but then works its way down through our "teachers," our politicians, the media, and even ourselves for letting the liberal charlatans pull one over on us. Shame on us all.

Here is one last example of this liberal movie manipulation of the masses from *Lincoln*: at one point, screenwriter Kushner and director Spielberg have Sally Field's Mary Todd Lincoln sitting in the Congressional gallery watching the proceedings and commenting on them with her African American housekeeper as the final vote tally is counted.

Interesting for the filmmakers to again project how this should have happened...except it did not. The intent of the filmmakers was clearly to show that women and minorities were equal or even better than the white men ruling the country at the time.

The fact is, all of God's children are equal and should always be treated as such. That said, as much as Mr. Spielberg and Mr. Kushner tried to squeeze their 2012 opinions and sensibilities into 1865, the reality was far from what they filmed and pawned off on the American people as "history."

Keep in mind, *Lincoln* is just *one* example of the *thousands* of movies, television programs, and books that seek to either twist history into a liberal perspective or indoctrinate American children and the population as a whole into believing that what is false and destructive is good and "progressive."

Like some of the most infamous dictators, tyrants, and murderers of the world's recent history, the far-left *is* succeeding at this massive re-education campaign. But at what cost to freedom?

* * *

Now, back to *actual* history.

Again, as all would agree, as abhorrent and inhumane as slavery was and is, as mentioned, it was a very complicated issue to grapple with before, during, and after the American Civil War.

Abraham Lincoln is considered by many to be one of our greatest presidents and an amazingly decent human being. That said, even for him, there was no easy "one size fits all" answer to slavery.

Said President Lincoln at the time:

My paramount object in this struggle is to save the Union, and is not either to save or to destroy slavery. If I could save the Union without freeing any slave I would do it, and if I could save it by freeing all the slaves I would do it; and if I could save it by free-ing some and leaving others alone, I would do that. What I do about slavery, and the colored race, I do because I believe it helps to save the Union: and what I forbear, I forbear because I do not believe it would help to save the Union. I shall do less whenever I shall believe what I am doing hurts the cause, and I shall do more whenever I shall believe doing more will help the cause.

So once again, aside from the subject of slavery, there were other real reasons why eleven states of the United States of America chose to secede from the Union.

* * *

At this point, I think it's critically important to mention that when the first group of southern states seceded from the Union, they did so peacefully, with no confrontation in mind, and—at least as far as they were concerned—in a totally legal and constitutional manner.

Because "history" is often written by the victors and because so little of substance and truth is taught in our schools today regard-ing the American Civil War, most students (if they are even aware of this part of our history), as well as most Americans (again, if they also are aware of the most tragic war fought in the history of our Republic), have no idea—that would be zero—that the South peacefully seceded from the United States of America.

* * *

During his first inaugural address to the nation on March 4, 1861, President Abraham Lincoln spoke to both the issue of slavery and the issue of "States Rights." In neither was he remotely unequivocal. In words written and intended for the people of the South to ease their growing apprehension, the new president said:

> I have no purpose, directly or indirectly, to interfere with the institution of slavery in the States where it exists. I believe I have no lawful right to do so, and I have no inclination to do so. Those who nominated and elected me did so with full knowledge that I had made this and many similar declarations and had never recanted them; and more than this, they placed in the platform for my acceptance, and as a law to themselves and to me, the clear and emphatic resolution which I now read:
>
> Resolved, That the maintenance inviolate of the rights of the States, and especially the right of each State to order and control its own domestic institutions according to its own judgment exclusively, is essential to that balance of power on which the perfection and endurance of our political fabric depend...

Those words from our sixteenth president sure sounded nice and were reassuring to the people and leaders of the South. And no doubt Abraham Lincoln meant every word right up until the moment he meant none of them.

Soon after the southern states of Alabama, Florida, Georgia, Louisiana, Mississippi, South Carolina, and Texas seceded from the Union (again, peacefully), the North began the conflict—never legally *declaring war* because they had no constitutional grounds to do so—with the new Confederate States of America.

Outraged by what they viewed as an illegal and unprovoked attack by the North, the states of Arkansas, North Carolina,

Tennessee, and Virginia quickly seceded from the Union to join forces with the Confederate States of America.

While many people consider the facts the enemy of their narrative or their agenda, it is still worth noting that the states of Alabama, Florida, Georgia, Louisiana, Mississippi, South Carolina, and Texas officially became the Confederate States of America in February of 1861.

Now, for those who care to do the math, that would be one month *before* Abraham Lincoln's appeasing and conciliatory words aimed at the people of the South, many of whom had *already* formed the Confederate States of America.

And yet, just a few short weeks after those assuring and comforting words delivered to the people of the South, Abraham Lincoln and his subordinates forced the Confederate States of America into a war they did not want.

Why? If he truly believed the words he wrote and delivered during his first inaugural, and if he truly believed his own words (which are quoted at the beginning of this book: "This country, with its institutions, belongs to the people who inhabit it. Whenever they shall grow weary of the existing government, they can exercise their constitutional right of amending it, or their revolutionary right to dismember or overthrow it."), why would he still push war upon the South and put in motion a conflict that would ultimately take the lives of 750,000 men?

Why?

There is no doubt that some scholars believe, with regard to the subject of constitutional safeguards against coercion by the central government, President Lincoln violated the Constitution by waging "war" on the states that peacefully seceded from the Union—a "war" that was not *officially* declared by Congress or President Lincoln. To do so would have recognized the Confederate States of

America as a legitimate government—something they would never allow to happen.

* * *

President Lincoln clearly understood *why* some states from the South seceded from the Union.

Chief among those reasons was "States Rights."

But understanding, caring, acknowledging, and allowing can sometimes mean different things to different people.

Abraham Lincoln may have been truly torn by the dilemma facing him and the nation, or he may have been completely resolute in his reading of the situation and his ultimate belief that the "Union" had to be preserved...at *any* cost.

No matter his ultimate state of mind at the time, it is clear that despite trying to calm the people of the South as he delivered his first inaugural, he had already made the decision—as excruciating as it may have been—to purposely ignore or put aside the argument of "States Rights" as a legitimate rationale for a state or states to leave the Union.

That said, it *was* a legitimate argument then, just as it is a legitimate argument now. It is crucial to the dialog we are now trying to create.

The argument for "States Rights"—both during the Civil War and now—were folded around the words, definition, and true meaning of the Tenth Amendment to the Bill of Rights. The amendment simply reads: "The powers not delegated to the United States by the Constitution, nor prohibited by it to the States, are reserved to the States respectively, or to the people."

Despite President Lincoln's tortured dilemma, the most logical interpretation of this amendment was that it was added to reinforce to the American people that the power of the federal government had limits and that the states and the people were free to also exercise their sovereign powers.

Central to this logical interpretation of the Tenth Amendment and central to the theme of this book is still the question President Lincoln wrestled with or chose to ignore back in 1861: Does the federal government have the power to force states to remain in the Union?

If you believe our own Declaration of Independence, the answer to that question is a firm *no*.

Says the parchment that is still sacred to tens of millions of Americans who cherish both its message and true Traditional Values:

> That these United Colonies are, and of Right ought to be Free and Independent States; that they are Absolved from all Allegiance to the British Crown, and that all political connection between them and the State of Great Britain, is and ought to be totally dissolved; and that as Free and Independent States, they have full Power to levy War, conclude Peace, contract Alliances, establish Commerce, and to do all other Acts and Things which Independent States may of right do.

Founding Father Samuel Adams of Massachusetts spoke to both the subject of "States Rights" as well as secession when he addressed the creation of our new Republic: "That each state retains its sovereignty, freedom, and independence, and every power, jurisdiction and right which is not by this confederation expressly delegated to the United States."

Samuel Adams was correct well over two hundred years ago when he made that critical point—just as we are right today to firmly believe that our federal government has gone too far not only in its naked grab for complete and unchallenged power, but also in its goal to tell us how to think, what is best for us, and the brain-washing of our children.

* * *

Several decades after Mr. Adams' critically important analysis, Lord Acton made two points that were both quite relevant to the time and even more relevant *now.*

The first: "Liberty is not a means to a higher political end. It is itself, the highest political end."

The second: "Socialism means slavery."

For those who may not quite remember, John Dalberg-Acton (1834–1902) was one of the most prominent historians and thinkers of his time. Most people know him for his quote: "Power tends to corrupt, and absolute power corrupts absolutely."

Aside from being a historian with a sixty-thousand-book personal library, Lord Acton also served as a member of Parliament in England.

Not surprisingly for those who knew him and understood his love of liberty and concern for the oppressed, he was fascinated by the American Civil War and sympathized greatly with the South—so much so that he entered into regular correspondence with General Robert E. Lee.

In one example of that now very historic correspondence, Lord Acton wrote to Robert E. Lee:

I saw in State Rights the only availing check upon the absolutism of the sovereign will, and secession filled me with hope, not as the destruction but as the redemption of Democracy. The institutions of your Republic have not exercised on the old world the salutary and liberating influence which ought to have belonged to them, by reason of those defects and abuses of principle which the Confederate Constitution was expressly and wisely calculated to remedy. I believed that the example of that great Reform would have blessed all the races of mankind by establishing true freedom purged of the native dangers and disorders of Republics. Therefore I deemed that you were fighting the battles of our liberty, our progress, and our civilization; and I mourn for the stake which was lost at Richmond more deeply than I rejoice over that which was saved at Waterloo.

General Robert E. Lee responded:

I yet believe that the maintenance of the rights and authority reserved to the states and to the people, not only essential to the adjustment and balance of the general system, but the safeguard to the continuance of a free government. I consider it as the chief source of stability to our political system, whereas the consolidation of the states into one vast republic, sure to be aggressive abroad and despotic at home, will be the certain precursor of that ruin which has overwhelmed all those that have preceded it.

One place Robert E. Lee almost assuredly started to form his strong beliefs regarding "States Rights" was at the United States Military Academy at West Point. It was there he and a number of officers who eventually fought for the South would have read the words of Mr. William Rawle, a man who was appointed United States District Attorney for Pennsylvania in 1791 by George Washington.

In *A View of the Constitution of the United States,* originally published in 1825 and available to Robert E. Lee as a student of West Point, Mr. Rawle addresses the always very topical—especially at the time—subject of secession. Wrote Mr. Rawle:

The secession of a state from the Union depends on the will of the people of such state . . . It depends on the State itself whether it will continue as a member of the Union. To deny this right would be inconsistent with the principles on which all our political systems are founded; which is, the people have, in all cases, a right to determine how they will be governed.

William Rawle's full text on this subject will follow later in this book, but this excerpt of his powerful words, which truly embraced liberty while adhering strictly to the salient themes of our founding documents, were known not only to Robert E. Lee, but to Abraham Lincoln as well. And yet, these two men of unrivaled dignity and character ended up on opposite sides of the most destructive conflict in the history of our Republic.

* * *

Beyond the beliefs of Lord Acton, Robert E. Lee, or even Abraham Lincoln are a few other cold, hard facts that speak to the right and legality of "States Rights" and secession:

First, no matter how it is defined or recorded by "historians" with a bias, the original thirteen colonies *seceded* from the British Empire. Others may call it whatever they like, but the fact is that our Founding Fathers—in the name of liberty and as their right as free human beings—saw secession from the British Crown as the *only* viable alternative to the growing oppression they faced.

Second, these original thirteen colonies entered the Union— often after tremendous lobbying where concessions were made to protect and guarantee their sovereignty—*voluntarily*. More importantly than that, *nowhere* in our founding documents does it say that the federal government has the right nor the power to *force* any state to remain in the Republic.

States like Rhode Island, New York, and Virginia spoke to this exact point and right as a condition to becoming part of the Union.

New York said in part: "That the powers of government may be reassumed by the People, whensoever it shall become necessary to their happiness."

The Commonwealth of Virginia declared: "We, the Delegates of the people of Virginia Do, in the name and in behalf of the People of Virginia, declare and make known that the powers granted under the Constitution being derived from the People of the United States may be resumed by them whensoever the same shall be perverted to their injury or oppression."

* * *

To close out this section, two points have to be noted:

If we do want to highlight consequential tipping points, then with regard to Abraham Lincoln's decision to wage war on the new Confederate States of America, there can be no doubt that once some countries in Europe began to recognize the Confederate States of America as a *sovereign nation,* he felt he had no choice but to act.

The other interesting point to at least ponder as a possible tipping point for the North waging its undeclared war against the South is that in 1860, the South produced 75 percent of *all* US exports. Many people in the North felt that without the South in the Union, the economy of the North *would simply collapse.*

CHAPTER 3

WHY A NEW NATION MUST BE FORMED

As to why *serious* people should give *serious* thought to forming a new nation built upon the rock solid principles of Traditional Values, the reasons have become endless and more catastrophic and compelling by the day. A number of examples will be highlighted in this chapter, above all being that our very government—as obvious to anyone who is honest and paying attention—is broken beyond all repair.

Shattered, in fact.

To this very point, former secretary of defense Robert Gates said the following in his 2014 bestselling memoir:

---

from *Duty: Memoirs of a Secretary at War* by **Robert Gates (Knopf, 2014)**

Such difficulties within the executive branch were nothing compared with the pain of dealing with Congress. Congress is best viewed from a distance—the farther the better—because up close, it is truly ugly. I saw most

---

of Congress as uncivil, incompetent at fulfilling their basic constitutional responsibilities (such as timely appropriations), micromanagerial, parochial, hypocritical, egotistical, thin-skinned and prone to put self (and re-election) before country...

I also bristled at what's become of congressional hearings, where rude, insulting, belittling, bullying and all too often highly personal attacks on witnesses by members of Congress violated nearly every norm of civil behavior. Members postured and acted as judge, jury and executioner. It was as though most members were in a permanent state of outrage or suffered from some sort of mental duress that warranted confinement or at least treatment for anger management.

Now keep in mind, these telling words come from one of *the* most respected civil servants in the history of our government. He is (or at least *was* until he dared to tell the truth in his own book) deeply admired by both sides of the aisle and served both broken political parties with great distinction during his incredibly impressive career.

Unfortunately for him—and all of us—he saw the political sausage made right before him and it made him sick to his stomach.

* * *

Unlike former secretary of defense Robert Gates however, for *well over one hundred million* Americans, the suicidal status quo of our nation is *just fine with them.* Whether they know it—or admit it—or not.

Who are these Americans? There are many examples we could cite, but to list just a few, they would be, again, the wealthy liberal powerbrokers who control most of the media, entertainment, and academia but snobbishly never live by the rules they foist upon the "unwashed masses." Some would be the often corrupt public employee unions, some would be the public employees who know the gold-plated benefits they are getting are unearned, unsustainable, and financially crippling their city, county, or state. Some would be the incompetent teachers who have given up on their students in favor of their own self-interests, and some would be the truly poor of America who are being deceived and simply don't have the time or energy to *find the truth.*

These are *your* fellow citizens who are either building and perfecting the All-Government Nanny state they deeply believe in or are too ignorant to know that what they are being told and the welfare crumbs they are being given as bribes are entrapping them within the independent thought-destroying tentacles of the All-Government.

No matter who they are, they *are* doomed because the reality is that the All-Government parasite is sucking the very life out of the host now known as the United States of America. But, when the parasite sucks the last bit of life out of the host, what happens then? They both eventually die. That, or the host for sure collapses from within and decays while the All-Government parasite jumps onto the flesh of another unsuspecting—or more likely intellectually incurious—victim.

Unfortunately, if you are one of the *tens of millions* of other Americans trying to fight this insanity and this moral affront to the dream of our Founding Fathers, those either thrilled with the status quo or ignorant of it are more than happy to take *you and your family* down with them.

And…as we all know…and as must be continually repeated…they are succeeding *beyond* their wildest dreams.

But, if you are one of those Americans who *can* think for themselves, who does believe in Traditional Values, and does believe— beyond a shadow of a doubt—that the United States of America is led by corrupt and incompetent politicians from both sides of the aisle either oblivious to the destruction they are wreaking, or worse, actively creating it for their own means, then what are *you* to do?

Do you join the other sheep in line and meekly go to the slaughter, or do you fight for your survival by reclaiming your rights as bestowed upon you by God and the words drafted and paid for in blood by our Founding Fathers?

No matter what the Obama White House says or those who have chosen to unethically and illegally do its bidding at the IRS, NSA, EPA, or other three-letter agencies of the United States government, we are *still* allowed—at the very least—to explore and discuss options that may be open to us.

While we do not exist in a complete Police State…yet…it is best we start a dialog now before even *that* is outlawed.

* * *

To highlight that very point, just after the actually not so shocking reelection of Barack Obama as President of the United States of America back in November 2012, conservative and Traditional Values–espousing national radio host Mark Levin attempted to sum up the feelings of those tens of millions of Americans who feel the country of President Obama and his allies no longer represents them or their values. He said in part:

from **"Mark Levin Gives 'Unvarnished Truth' On Romney Loss," RealClearPolitics.com, November 2012**

We conservatives, we do not accept bipartisanship in the pursuit of tyranny. Period...We are the alternative. We will resist. We're not going to surrender to this. We will not be passive, we will not be compliant in our demise...

Now to be sure, Mr. Levin is right to articulate his outrage as it exactly mirrors the outrage and despair of millions of us—just as he is correct when he highlights the specific point that "[w]e conservatives, we do not accept bipartisanship in the pursuit of Tyranny."

Where he is partially wrong, however—in my humble opinion—is when he mentions that more than fifty-seven million people voted against Barack Obama and "tyranny," and those "who choose tyranny over liberty...do not get to dictate to us under our Constitution."

Well...two critical points regarding Mr. Levin's statement: First, sadly, tragically, and dangerously, those who do "choose tyranny over liberty" *do* "get to dictate to us under our Constitution." They absolutely do.

That's the whole point of this book and hopefully...this movement.

They grabbed the reins of power long ago and have steered the cart into the path of certain death for liberty, a smaller, less intrusive government, the rule of law, and our very futures.

While Mr. Levin and tens of millions of us wish this were not the case, the unassailable fact of the matter is that it *is* the case. Those who believe in and promote the policies of the All-Government Nanny state *do* get to dictate to us under our Constitution.

Why?

First and foremost, because they have *zero respect* for the Constitution and deliberately and repeatedly ignore or subvert this sacred document whenever it suits their needs (as President Obama and his administration have demonstrated time and again) precisely so they *can* dictate to us. It is all part of their greater master plan.

Next, they get to do so because, as stressed earlier, they control the public megaphones of the country. By that, I mean they have almost *exclusive* control over our media, our educational system, and our entertainment outlets. They know that if you tell a lie often enough, it becomes fact to most Americans. And those continually pushing the destructive policies of the All-Government Nanny state have become exceptionally good at telling lies on a regular basis.

Next, while Mr. Levin is right that over fifty-seven million Americans voted against the corrosive policies of Barack Obama, how many of them are truly willing to stand up and be counted?

As in the beginning of this book, it might be best to cut that number in half and assume that approximately thirty million Americans—out of a nation of between 330 million to 400 million depending upon how many illegal aliens permanently reside in the country—would be willing to at least *strongly consider* standing up for themselves and their families in the face of such tyranny.

Next, while Mr. Levin also stresses that "[w]e are the alternative. We will resist. We are not going to surrender to this. We will not be passive. We will not be compliant in our demise," I believe he is wrong in this case.

Again—and this bears repeating time and again—most of our fellow citizens *will* surrender to this. They *will* be passive. They *will* be compliant to their own demise. Not only will they do all of these things, but they *are* doing all of these things.

Why?

Simple.

Americans of faith who believe in Traditional Values are, of course, often some of the nicest people you will ever meet—nice sometimes to a flaw.

And guess what? The far-left not only *knows* it, but is *counting* on Americans of faith and values to continually turn the other cheek when attacked or when their rights are threatened or continually watered down.

Again, the far-left zealots and politicians in it for themselves not only know this, but factor the "civility" and "politeness" into their strategy.

More often than not, many conservatives and Americans of faith will just take it. Oh, they may scream about the injustice of it all and call a few radio programs or write some letters to the editor, but at the end of the day, many will simply wring their hands and remain silent. It's what they often do. They are naturally polite and respectful of the "rights" of others.

Many on the left not only laugh at such politeness, but they also see it as a weakness and as an opening to attack. And attack they do. Continually, viciously, and usually until they achieve complete destruction and capitulation—at least in their minds.

If they feel conservatives, Christians, or "evil" corporate America are threatening—or more likely *exposing* one of their pet politically correct Nanny-state causes as a fraud and a huge waste of taxpayer dollars—they will come after their targets with a vengeance. Again, *any* means justifies the All-Government totalitarian end they are seeking.

They will boycott. They will picket. They will march. They will harass. They will hack. They will invade your neighborhood or home. They will spit. They will scream. They will—as they have done in the past—throw feces, urine, blood, and used tampons. They will infiltrate. And they will ultimately physically attack—*or worse*—should one care to remember back to the days of Obama mentor and alleged terrorist Bill Ayers.

Bottom line: while conservatives and Americans of faith do the polite and civil thing, many on the far-left will employ a scorched earth policy until they declare victory in the name of social engineering and socialist dogma over common sense, the rule of law, and liberty—in every sense of that word.

Standing on principle and fighting to preserve freedom and our vanishing way of life is not easy. *Obviously.* But, as mentioned, there *are* at least a core group of thirty million Americans who share this vision and who are willing to stand shoulder-to-shoulder to try and make the vision a reality, no matter the lies told or the tactics used to silence them.

Some very, very good Americans have been beaten into submission by the disciples of the All-Government Nanny state.

They have... but *we*... have not.

* * *

That flickering light of hope that we do see in the far distance does come from the eyes of millions of Americans who *do* believe in Traditional Values and who *do* believe that the country of their youth—the country they fought to defend, the country of their dreams, and most of all, the country they wanted to turn over to their children and grandchildren—is in a death spiral from which there will be no recovery.

It is a light entirely fueled by the knowledge that there will be no alternative unless *they* finally take the matter into their hands.

As to *why* they think that way, what follows are just a few specifics that detail how wide, deep, inherently corrosive, and unstoppable the policies of the All-Government Nanny state have become:

FAITH:

As talked about earlier—and a reality we must *never* lose sight of—there is a systematic *attack* on faith, belief in God, and most especially those who *believe* in God, by the far-left and its agents in the media, academia, entertainment, and "science."

While these attacks do occasionally and generically touch all faiths and *any* belief in God, for the most part, they are aimed squarely at the *Christian faith* and *Christians.*

For the far-left, attacks upon Christianity are always in season and are viewed by the liberals who perpetrate them as a *blood sport.*

On this very point, Roman Catholic Cardinal Raymond Burke—the Chief Justice of the Vatican—went out of his way in 2014 to single out Barack Obama as a person openly hostile to the Christian faith.

Said the cardinal in part:

> from **"Cardinal Burke on faith, the right to life, and the family: English exclusive," LifeSiteNews.com, March 2014**
>
> It is true that the policies of the President of the United States have become progressively *more hostile toward Christian civilization*. He appears to be a totally secularized man who *aggressively promotes anti-life and*

> *anti-family policies...* Now he wants to restrict the exercise of freedom of religion to freedom of worship, that is, he holds that one is free to act according to his conscience within the confines of his place of worship but that, once the person leaves the place of worship, *the Government can constrain him to act against his rightly-formed conscience,* even in the most serious of moral questions... In a Democracy, such a lack of awareness *is deadly.* It leads to the loss of freedom which a democratic government exists to protect...

For more proof of this, we have Barack Obama–supporting, ultra-wealthy, ultra-liberal, proudly atheist, and Christian and Catholic–smearing Seth MacFarlane becoming executive producer of the newly launched "Science" program titled *Cosmos.*

The atheist cartoon guy is now in charge of *Cosmos*? What's next? The far-left picks convicted sex offenders to run nursery schools?

No matter *what* they say, the premise of Mr. MacFarlane's show will *only* be to bash Christians while working overtime to prove that God does not exist.

For a more "mainstream" example of this hateful and twisted bias, look no further than the 2014 Grammy Awards.

That would be the broadcast where pop singer Katy Perry (the daughter of a minister) was dressed as a witch and then burned at the stake while more than thirty gay couples were *legally* married behind her in a deliberate attempt by the producers to mock and insult those who happen to believe in the sanctity of traditional marriage.

After watching this perverse representation of far-left theology, then University of Alabama All-American quarterback A. J. McCarron sent out a tweet saying: "Is it me or do some of the

Grammy performances so far seem to be really demonic?? Looks like there is a lot of evil in the world."

How right Mr. McCarron was and remains. Not only is there "a lot of evil in the world," but a great deal of that "Evil" resides right here in the United States of America.

So much so that it is about to accomplish what all our combined enemies could not: completely vanquishing the nation created by our Founding Fathers.

It seems every single day, the questions before us become: Do we succumb to this evil? Do we accept it? Do we allow it to lay waste to everything we hold sacred?

Or...

Do we fight back in the name of our faith, in the name of liberty, the rule-of-law, and on behalf of all those we love and hold dear?

As outlined, by our estimate, at least *10 percent* of the nation is willing to fight back in one form or another in the name of their freedom and their faith.

The next question then becomes: Has that ten percent reached the point of no return?

On this very subject, former director of communications for President Ronald Reagan and bestselling author and columnist Patrick J. Buchanan said:

---

from " 'Duck Dynasty' and the New Blacklist,"
Creators.com, December 2013

. . . In the 21st Century, biblical Christianity is persona non grata. No, this is not the America we grew up in. And it is becoming less so...Worldwide too,

> Christianity...seems in a long retreat. Receding slowly in America, and moribund in Europe, Christianity is undergoing merciless persecutions in Africa and the Middle East—from Nigeria to Egypt, Syria, and Iraq.

Mr. Buchanan is one of the true Patriots of our time—a voice of reason and honor to be admired, defended, and heeded. Tragically for us all, fewer and fewer people are paying attention.

DISCRIMINATION BY HOMOSEXUALS AND HOMOSEXUAL MARRIAGE:

As stressed earlier, we *are* all God's children. Period.

That said—as highlighted previously—the small but increasingly powerful homosexual lobby has taken it upon itself to not only impose their definition of morals upon the 98 percent of the rest of the nation, but to practice outright discrimination at the same time.

First, as discussed, as all but a tiny percentage have come to experience, life is very hard and can often be beyond cruel. With this knowledge, most Christians—and most people, whether they embrace a faith or not—simply want people to be happy. All people.

But again, what happens when a tiny minority with a disproportionally massive influence within the media, entertainment, and academia—thanks in large part to the *illegal* tactic of the hiring discrimination they employ at every opportunity—can successfully dictate to, and vilify, well over 90 percent of the population of our nation?

Let's see...who could be named as a poster child for this type of unethical behavior? How about the aforementioned Seth MacFarlane? Not only is he an atheist who bashes Christians whenever possible, but he is one of the strongest advocates for homosexual marriage there is in the country. How did he make it into the industry?

Mr. MacFarlane is certainly entitled to support any legitimate cause. That said, maybe he can *honestly* answer how the homosexual lobby—which only represents 2 to 3 percent of the population *maximum* based on a number of credible studies—can wield such power and influence over the rest of us?

As an example of that power and influence, let's look at the world of "entertainment" for a moment.

A few years ago, the recent announcement from DC Comics that, for reasons of political correctness, they were making their Green Lantern character gay was met with a yawn. As was the recent same-sex marriage in *Archie Comics* and the upcoming same-sex marriage in a Marvel *X-Men* comic. More recently, we have a Viking character in *How to Train your Dragon 2* coming out as gay.

Catching the trend? The far-left does want to brain-wash young children as early and as repeatedly as possible and they are doing so across their rainbow spectrum.

According to a former high-level Disney executive I spoke with, this is all part of a greater "indoctrination campaign" to make those opposed to same-sex marriage and the gay lifestyle *"seem out of the mainstream or even bigoted."*

This same executive told me the Disney company, most especially through its "children's" programing on the Disney Channel and Disney XD, have been subtly and not so subtly pushing the gay agenda for years.

This executive said one of the overt ways the Disney writers and the Disney company pushed the gay agenda—aside from now openly gay characters—was during its first Disney Games for Change campaign. According to my source, during one of the sports competitions between the child actors from the various

Disney programs, a Gay Pride flag was hung from one of the ropes and televised as it was hoisted.

They also push a gay agenda and gay pride on the Disney programs by making sure the colors of the Gay Pride flag are incorporated into as many shots as possible. If one were to watch the actual Disney shows on a regular basis, it's obvious this former executive is correct. The colors are purposely woven in—as a wink and a nod to the gay community, according to the former executive—to posters in the background, hats, rings, shirts, stacked cups, you name it. Once you start looking for them, you actually lose count of how many ways they're incorporated into the background.

This former executive tells me this practice has now spread not only to the Nickelodeon Network, but to national advertising in general. Look for it. Be it Coca-Cola or others, it has become a sophomoric and childish way for gay and liberal straight writers to make a "gay pride" statement while giggling at how clever they are.

How proud they must be...except...according to the former executive, throughout the years, more and more gay executives, writers, or producers—be they at Disney or elsewhere—have engaged in outright illegal discrimination to allegedly "right the wrongs of the past." So much so that, by some estimates, more than *60 percent of all writers on sit-coms in Hollywood are now gay*. By *any* definition, that is outright discrimination.

Where is *that* story on the network news or in our top newspapers?

Whoops. How foolish of me to ask. The executives at these media outlets support and in fact encourage and utilize such illegal discrimination in the name of "diversity"—as long as there are no conservatives or practicing Christians on the "must hire" list.

Another item that won't make the news: the majority of the male employees at the Disney theme parks in the United States are now gay, according to the former Disney executive. How does that happen?

Unfortunately, this type of blatant and purposely "in your face" discrimination fits a pattern for the liberal ideology. In today's America, *only* liberals are allowed to discriminate, and they do so with a vengeance. They discriminate against conservatives and Christians at the majority of our universities and colleges, against straight conservatives in Hollywood, or against conservatives and Christians at the top 100 newspapers or national "news" networks.

Sadly, such discrimination is pervasive, growing, and undeniable.

I have often said that *human nature dictates that we embrace the truth right up until the moment it reflects poorly upon ourselves or our cause.* The absolute truth of the matter here is that nobody condemns discrimination louder than liberals. Nobody. Except when they *willingly* practice it to further their agenda. Then discrimination simply becomes a means to an end.

Going back to the Disney company and the Disney Channel for a moment, though: they have never hidden the fact that they are far-left—Michelle Obama has appeared on every Disney show so often it seems she is under contract to the Mouse—or that they strongly support the gay agenda. Quite the opposite, actually. They are quite proud of their corporate agenda. That is most certainly their right, but along with that "right" comes responsibility.

Part of that responsibility is to obey the law and not discriminate against well over 90 percent of our population, with the greater responsibility being to not indoctrinate America's innocent children into a liberal ideology that trashes faith while charging that those who believe in traditional marriage—again, well over 90 percent of the population—are bigots or "evil" under the dictates of the Disney liberal doctrine.

This is not to say there are not independent and honest thinkers within the liberal or gay community. With regard to the plight of our country in general, well-known feminist and openly gay author and professor Camille Paglia made some very accurate observations that infuriate many of her fellow liberals and many from the gay community. So much so that—no surprise—some want her independent and common sense thought *censored*. A liberal black list. Who would have imagined?

Said the never shy Ms. Paglia in part:

- "What you're seeing now is how a civilization commits suicide."
- "The entire elite class now, in finance, in politics and so on, none of them have military service—hardly anyone, there are a few. But there is no prestige attached to it anymore. That is a recipe for disaster."
- "These people don't think in military ways, so there's this illusion out there that people are basically nice, people are basically kind, if we're just nice and benevolent to everyone they'll be nice too. They literally don't have any sense of evil or criminality."
- "I believe that every person, male and female, needs to be in a protective mode at all times of alertness to potential danger. The world is full of potential attacks, potential disasters."
- "Primary education is a crock..."
- "Michelle Obama's going on: 'Everybody must have college.' Why? Why? What is the reason why everyone has to go to college? Especially when college is so utterly meaningless right now, it has no core curriculum."
- "Obamacare is a monstrosity."
- "Global Warming is a religious dogma."[1]

* * *

---

1 Many of these quotes were featured in "Camille Paglia: A Feminist Defense of Masculine Virtues" from an issue in the *Wall Street Journal* from December 2013, written by Bari Weiss.

From the clearly true observations of Ms. Paglia, we jump back to yet *another* reason millions of Americans who believe in Traditional Values and traditional marriage have given up on the United States of America: our "government" has enabled the homosexual lobby to win the war against gay marriage.

Make no mistake, your "leaders"—and, quite tragically, that includes a fair number of people in the clergy—have waved the white flag on this issue. Not only have they surrendered their rights, but, totally without our permission, they have surrendered *ours* as well.

Because the homosexual lobby does have a hand on the megaphones of our country—thanks again to the discrimination they and the other liberals who support them practice on a regular basis—they have been remarkably successful in forcing politicians to redefine "marriage."

Along with bullying, intimidating, or guilting the weak or morally corrupt politicians into bending to their will, they orchestrated a very successful campaign to demonize Americans of faith who happen to support traditional marriage.

Thanks solely to this campaign by the homosexual lobby, there is now a growing climate of intolerance of, and discrimination against, Americans who happen to believe that marriage is and must remain a union between one man and one woman.

As an American business operator and job creator and provider, if you dare *not* to cater to homosexual marriage for reasons *only* related to your faith, the homosexual lobby and all who support it in and out of government will do all in their exponentially growing power to put you out of business, prosecute you, or both.

Welcome to the upside-down world that is the current United States of America.

* * *

As the very topic of Christian businesses being forced by their own government to provide goods and services for gay marriages raged on, Erick Erickson, the creator of the exceptional site *Red State* and one of the leading voices of conservative thought in the media, made this very necessary and correct point in a column:

> ### from "Yes, Jesus Would Bake A Cake for a Gay Person" RedState.com, February 2014
>
> Jesus Christ would absolutely bake a cake for a gay person. He'd bake a cake for a straight person. He'd bake a cake for a girl, a boy, a person who isn't sure what they are, a black person, a white person—Jesus would bake that cake *if it, in some way large or small,* drew that person closer to Him...
>
> ... The disagreement comes on one issue only—should a Christian provide goods and services to a gay wedding. That's it. We're not talking about serving a meal at a restaurant. We're not talking about baking a cake for a birthday party. We're talking about a wedding, which millions of Christians view as a sacrament of the faith and other, mostly Protestant Christians, view as a relationship ordained by God to reflect a holy relationship.
>
> This slope is only slippery if you grease it with hypotheticals not in play.
>
> There are Christians who have no problem providing goods and services for a gay marriage. Some of them are fine with gay marriage. Some of them think

gay marriage is wrong, but they still have no problem providing goods and services.

Other Christians, including a significant number of Catholic and Protestant preachers, believe that a gay marriage is a sinful corruption of a relationship God himself ordained. Because they try to glorify God through their work, they believe they cannot participate in a wedding service. Yes, because they believe they are glorifying God in their work and view it as a ministry, they view providing goods and services as a way to advance, even in a small way, God's kingdom.

Herein lies the dispute of the day. The latter group does not stand in the way of the former group providing cakes, flowers, and pictures for a gay wedding. *Some of the former, however, believe the government should compel the latter group to violate their conscience.* They only see the transaction through the customer's eyes as if the vendors are passive participants.

That's the problem.

We are not talking about race. We are not talking about restaurants. We are talking about a specific ceremony people of faith believe God himself created and ordained. Should the state force people to violate their conscience in that regard?

It is not staggering that there are aggrieved gay rights activists who think the state should be able to force people to recognize as normal that which most Christians view as sinful. *What is staggering is the number of Christians who apparently think the State has the right to decide and enforce this issue.*

You might think Jesus would bake a cake for a gay wedding. I think you are wrong. *I do not think Jesus Christ would participate in the ratification of a sin—and a marriage between two people of the same sex is a sin.* Are you really going to tell the millions of Christians in the United States who think otherwise that not only are they wrong, but the state should be able to force your opinion of what Jesus would do on them? In your pride, you might think 2000 years of Christian orthodoxy and the majority of practicing Christians in the world today are wrong—but don't think among people of practicing Christian faith you are in the majority.

I understand if you are not a believer and define yourself based on your sexual preference that you think the government should legitimize you by forcing others to treat you in a particular way. *But it boggles my mind to think any Christian should want the government to force their view of Christianity on another believer.*

If you think the government should be able to force Christians to provide goods and services to a gay wedding or risk losing their business, why not command a preacher's service? If a Christian baker cannot opt out, why should a preacher be able to opt out? And why not take from churches their tax exempt status if they fail to participate?

Christians should serve. But the government should not force them to.[2]

---

2   Used with permission from Erick Erickson.

Alas, with each passing day, the "government" *is* forcing "them" and us to do more and more things against our will, against our principles, and against our faith. At what point does a "government" morph into a totalitarian "dictatorship?"

US IMMIGRATION "POLICY":

Who made the following foolish but fearful remarks that reminded so many Traditional Values Americans why they have lost complete faith in the system?:

> ...two of the safest cities in America...are on the border with Mexico. And of course, the reason is, we've proved that Communism works. If you give everybody a good government job, there's no crime.

Those words were spoken by liberal Democrat Congressman Joe Garcia from Florida. That would be the same Joe Garcia who also became a YouTube sensation for being caught on film picking and then eating his own earwax.

Luckily for the late-night comedians but sadly for the nation, this liberal Democrat with an eclectic eating habit does not seem to know first grade math. If, as he states, "you give everyone a good government job" then who is left to pay those salaries?

As *all* government workers get paid from the taxes taken from hardworking Americans *not* on the government dime, then how would this utopian dream proving "Communism works" actually sustain itself?

Not only does Mr. Garcia seem to think Communism is the answer for full-employment, but he is also one of the leading voices for amnesty as it relates to the immigration policies of the United States.

Instead of "US Immigration Policy," maybe the politicians like Mr. Garcia who *pretend* to run our country should simply be honest and call it the "We let anyone in the country who we think will vote for us in exchange for entitlement bribes or at least not vote against us because the other party says we are anti-them" policy.

Aside from being disgraceful and greatly injurious to our nation—putting out a welcome mat for terrorists—it's also a highly flawed strategy.

To be sure, the Democratic Party—to the detriment of millions of African Americans and Hispanic Americans—has rightfully come to be known as the party that purposely gives little or no respect to minority America because they rightfully assume—based in part on the taxpayer–funded entitlement crumbs they sweep off the table toward them—that the majority of minority Americans who do vote *will* vote for them.

Consequently—despite what various minority American "leaders" say while working overtime to sustain their egos or fill their own bank accounts—this demographic has been all but ignored and taken completely for granted by the Democrats for decades and allowed—and actually *forced* by the liberal policies of the All-Government Nanny state—to fall deeper and deeper into poverty and dependency.

Please correct me—or fire up the "Hate Express"—if I'm wrong, but isn't that the very definition of a modern-day "plantation" mentality?

On the other side of that coin is the idea that, for decades, too many Republican "leaders" felt the Democrats had a lock on the minority American vote and therefore ignored this important—and mostly *conservative*—community rather than engage them in intelligent dialog and debate and offer them alternatives to the insults being disguised as "help" the Democrats were offering.

Today, as *both* political parties shamefully troll for the votes, or approval, of the illegal aliens and their relatives residing within the United States, they have missed the real answer standing before them the whole time: the tens of millions of *legal* immigrants to our nation who *do* vote and who *do* feel they have been marginalized or outright ignored as Democrats and Republicans pander to those who entered our nation illegally.

What might surprise these Democrats and Republicans, should they ever bother to reach out to this critical voting bloc, is that millions of them are in fact *Hispanic Americans* who strongly feel— and feel quite proudly—that because they obeyed the laws of our nation, that they stood in line as required by law, that they enthusiastically studied the history of our nation so they could one day become citizens, *every other immigrant* should do the same. Period.

Because Democrats and Republicans tie themselves in knots trying to please the proponents of illegal immigration from Mexico and Latin America, they also fail to remember *the millions of other legal and proud immigrants* to our country from nations outside of Latin America—immigrants from countries like Russia, Korea, India, the European Union, the Middle East, and Indonesia; immigrants who did all that our nation asked of them to become legal citizens; immigrants who *do* vote in our elections, as well as theirs; and immigrants who also feel betrayed by both political parties.

This subject serves to further illustrate why millions of Americans feel so dejected about their country and have lost all hope that politicians from either side of the aisle will advocate for them and their Traditional Values.

To cement their viewpoint is the complete sellout by so many Republican "leaders" on immigration and amnesty on behalf of those who *did* break the laws of our nation.

Alabama Republican Senator Jeff Sessions spoke to this sellout and pandering-induced about-face by so many of his colleagues in Congress in early 2014.

In an excellent column for *USA Today*, Senator Sessions pointed out that the GOP should remember that their first duty is to "help struggling Americans find good work and rising wages," and not succumb to the temptation to troll for Hispanic-American votes which are never going to come their way. The Traditional Values–espousing senator from Alabama called it a "national emergency." It is actually worse than that. It's a national disgrace.

To be sure, many or most of the illegal aliens sneaking into our nation are good people just trying to provide for their families. That said, they are "good people" who still broke our laws and illegally entered our country. Again, why have borders if we have no intention of enforcing them. Let's just make the planet Earth one multicultural country with no borders.

As of now, our nation admits one million immigrants per year. President Obama, his allies, and, sadly, a growing number of Republicans want to increase that number to three million per year or thirty million less-skilled workers flooding into our country to compete for the dwindling number of jobs.

You think technology is eliminating the need for the American worker now? Just wait until 2024 and see what happens.

The American worker is already getting crushed by this problem and to Senator Sessions' point, it is only being made dramatically worse by politicians with no principles.

As we all witnessed, despite the best efforts of Senator Sessions and others, the GOP *did choose* to side with the Obama White House in delivering a crushing hammer blow to the middle class—no real surprise to anyone keeping an eye on them the last few years.

About the same time Senator Jeff Sessions wrote his column, the always colorful, always honest, and almost always spot-on Ann Coulter echoed the words of the senator from Alabama but in a much more direct and attention-getting way. Said Ms. Coulter in part:

---

from "GOP crafts plan to wreck country, lose voters," HumanEvents.com, January 2014

As House Republicans prepare to *sell out the country on immigration* this week, Phyllis Schlafly has produced a stunning report on how immigration is changing the country…Citing surveys from the Pew Research Center, the Pew Hispanic Center, Gallup, NBC News, Harris polling, the Annenberg Policy Center, overwhelmingly demonstrates that merely *continuing our current immigration policies spells doom for the Republican Party.*

Ms. Coulter then correctly closes her column by saying: "Sorry, Americans. You lose."

She is absolutely correct. On this issue and so many others, we *have* lost and there is *no* going back.

THE SECOND AMENDMENT AND THE RIGHT TO BEAR ARMS:

First, if you don't think the Obama administration and its numerous allies in the media, academia, and entertainment have been crafting and pushing an agenda that would eventually take *all* guns out of the hands of law-abiding Americans, then it's time for your wake-up call.

Next, let's take a look at that Second Amendment, written and affirmed by our Founding Fathers, which has the far-left in such a foul and dictatorial mood:

A well-regulated Militia, being necessary to the security of a free State, the right of the people to keep and bear Arms, shall not be infringed.

That's it, but those *twenty-seven carefully chosen words* and the escalating attacks upon them by the far-left serve as yet one more reason why tens of millions of Americans have lost faith in their government and their "leadership."

One person who has declared war on the Second Amendment and those twenty-seven words is Barack Obama–supporting movie producer Harvey Weinstein.

Said the ultra-wealthy yet far-left—when it suits his purposes— Mr. Weinstein to radio personality Howard Stern: "I don't think we need guns in this country, and I hate it. I think the NRA is a disaster area...I shouldn't say this but I'll tell you, Howard. I'm going to make a movie with Meryl Streep, and we're going to take this head-on and they're going to wish they weren't alive after I'm done with them."

Mr. Weinstein—as reported—then contradicted himself when he told Mr. Stern that he would have wanted the Jewish citizens in Nazi Germany during World War II to have guns and to use them.

What Mr. Weinstein doesn't seem to know or remember is that thanks to the *Nazi government creating a gun registry* with names and addresses, they were able to confiscate all the guns from the Jewish citizens of Nazi Germany before and during their attempted genocidal extermination of all who practiced that faith. Additionally, the Gestapo issued a directive forbidding the issuance of gun permits to Jews. Worse than that, the Gestapo also used these same lists to pull people from their homes and place them into labor camps.

Knowing that, why would Mr. Weinstein want to confiscate guns now from law-abiding citizens or ban them at all? Surely, there are better examples and policies to follow.

* * *

With those totalitarian tactics of *Nazi Germany* in mind, it is more than fair to ask now what constitutes a "Police State" and who would serve as the propagandists of such an abuse of governmental power?

Speaking of "creating a gun registry," one candidate for what Vladimir Lenin once referred to as "Useful Idiots" might be *Civitas* Media, based in North Carolina. With approximately 100 publications and more than 1.6 million readers, it does have influence.

In 2014, one of its top executives suggested building a "state-by-state database" of concealed weapon permit holders. *Chilling* in its concept, to say the least.

Fortunately, it seems that one of their own employees found the project so disturbing and un-American that he leaked the memo from the *Civitas* executive to Fox News.

Once discovered, the executive and his protectors in management tried the "nothing to see here" routine with no success by claiming they suddenly had no plans to publish the list.

Michael Hammond, a spokesperson for the highly respected and influential Gun Owners of America, found that statement from *Civitas* hard to believe. "Why would a newspaper chain go to the trouble of compiling a list if they had no interest in publishing it? Isn't that what newspapers do? It's clear this newspaper chain doesn't intend to do good," he told Fox News.

Said Chad Baus, a spokesperson from Buckeye Firearms Association, to Fox News with regard to *Civitas* having their hand caught in the cookie jar: "They are saying they're not going to publish the list, but once the list is compiled, what are they going to do with it?...Our goal is to raise awareness because each and every time a newspaper organization does this type of thing, the public reacts very strongly to it. And yes, we do want it stopped...There's no other purpose for creating these lists but to target and victimize gun owners...There are many people who choose for that information not to be public, whether for employment reasons or family politics. Many law-abiding people don't want that information to be public."

Amplifying that much-needed point, Andrew Arulanandam, a spokesman for the multi-million member National Rifle Association, told Fox News: "There is no legitimate need for any news organization to compile a list of law-abiding citizens who have concealed carry permits. There are serious security concerns. For example, some people who have carry permits have stalkers and these news organizations are essentially providing a lighted pathway to the homes of these individuals."

Beyond wanting to take all the guns out of the hands of law-abiding citizens, the Obama administration is buying hundreds of millions of rounds (bullets) for the various "police" forces it *directly* controls. Why?

As the saying goes, "If this doesn't make your skin crawl, it's on too tight."

We *are* in deep trouble.

GLOBAL WARMING:

Sorry. I forgot that with the temperature of the planet *not* rising over the last twenty years and with some very credible and *not* compromised scientists from around the world even speaking of a lengthy upcoming period of "Global Cooling"—which would be infinitely more harmful and lethal to humankind—the far-left zealots who worship at the altar of their "Global Warming Religion" decided—so they did not continue to publicly look like the fools they are—to move the goal posts back significantly and change the name of "Global Warming" to "Climate Change."

See how convenient that is? Now, no matter what happens with the weather, be it brutal cold, nonstop blizzards, heat waves, or even biblical locusts descending upon the Midwest, they can smugly look down their noses at the common sense–believing, hardworking Americans before them and say: "See, this is all *your* fault. Humans cause all of this and we need to *shut down* American industry and pour billions of your rapidly dwindling tax dollars into useless 'green' initiatives pushed by our ultra-wealthy messiahs, Barack Obama and Al Gore, so they may please their political donors or corporate benefactors so *we* can save the planet. Oh, and in case you are too stupid to know—as we have long proclaimed—the science *is settled* on this argument."

To that very point of liberal "scientists" daring to say any science is *settled*, bestselling author and syndicated columnist Charles Krauthammer had this to say about their attempts to *silence* and *censor* not only *his* views, but also common sense and job-protecting dissent in general:

from **"Heating up: Climate change advocates try to silence Krauthammer," Fox News, February 2014**

When it comes to free speech, they don't even hide it anymore. Now they proudly want certain arguments banished from discourse. The next step is book burning. So the question of the day is: Can you light a Kindle? Is there anything *more anti-scientific* than scientific truths being determined by petition and demonstration?

Today, the twisted math of the far-left is clear: "Open-mind and logical skepticism = Climate Denier."

How "progressive."

PUBLIC-EMPLOYEE UNION GREED:

Almost all Americans who cherish Traditional Values know or are learning that their particular city, county, or state is on the brink of complete financial ruin and collapse. More than that, they know *exactly* why: the naked, beyond-selfish, and totally unrepentant greed of the public-employee unions and many of their employees are to blame.

Most of these employees flat-out know their wildly unfunded pensions and benefits are crippling the municipalities or public services they work for and are robbing the life savings of every taxpayer who contributes to municipalities.

But guess what? Many don't care.

No one who believes in Traditional Values would find such an obscene scenario acceptable.

The far-left and their enablers in the media like to portray the hardworking business owners and CEOs who create *all* the private-sector jobs in our country as "elitist, out-of-touch, and evil."

The irony in that foolish accusation is the *far-left* created and now protects the ultimate *"privileged class"* in our country.

Sadly and insultingly, many of the employees of this "privileged class" like to hide behind their corrupt unions and try to justify this gluttonous greed as *deserved compensation* for the "measly salaries" they are paid.

Give me a break.

Every honest American knows that if one of these public service jobs was offered tomorrow with *zero pension*—jobs that pay from $20,000 to well over $100,000 per year—*thousands* of the unemployed would line up immediately and consider themselves *blessed* with good fortune if they landed one.

Because most of the mainstream media are in the tank for the Obama White House or the liberal "cause," you will not hear nor read in their outlets that the estimate of the national pension debt has tripled to more than $3 trillion. That's trillion with a "T."

If we want to look at the poster child for public-employee pension greed, then we have to look no further than the state of California.

While the following statistic is incomprehensible and virtually impossible to believe for even the most jaded American, it is shockingly true: of every public dollar the state of California collects, 80 cents of it (or more) has to go to pay for the unfunded pensions and benefits of its public employees.

How much is the "Golden State" in the red? Realistic estimates have it at about $740 billion. To put *that* number into some kind of understandable perspective, the entire annual budget for the entire state is about $80 billion.

This reality is not only suicidal, but it's replicating itself in *almost every state, county, and city in the nation.* These unfunded public-employee pensions are strangling the economic life out of our nation.

After falsely and ridiculously screaming that "no one would take these 'low-paying' government jobs without a pension," the next line of defense offered by the public-employee union "leadership" is that "our employees paid into this pension system and therefore have earned their pension."

Okay. Fine. Then let's figure out *exactly* how much each public employee paid into his or her pension fund over the years (usually 0–3 percent of their salary), and then pay them *exactly* that amount in retirement and in health-care benefits and then not *one penny more.*

Will that ever happen? No.

Why? 1) These public-employee unions "own" much of the Democratic Party and 2) a great many politicians from *both sides of the aisle* are planning on cashing in on *exactly* these type of pensions.

All this insatiable greed is coming at (and causing) a time when the stated *national debt* is approximately *$17 trillion dollars*—a number that may not even come close to reflecting the actual national debt, which could be *ten times* that amount when unfunded liabilities and bankrupt, bailout-craving states are factored in.

Knowing that, *why wouldn't* Americans who believe in personal responsibility and Traditional Values want to start over someplace fresh? *Say, a new nation of their own.*

OBAMACARE:

Question: With regard to Barack Obama's signature socialist program, who said the following?

- "It's darn sure un-American."
- "Mr. Obama's plan is really bad for America."

- "It doesn't work for patients. It doesn't work for families. It doesn't work for doctors. And it certainly doesn't work for employers or employees."
- "Obamacare will destroy the American health-care system."
- "It's already destroyed jobs, it's already destroyed our economy, and if it stays in place…it's going to *destroy America*."

Answer: All highly accomplished *American doctors*.

Enough said.

* * *

Just *one* of these issues is enough to make Traditional Values–espousing Americans throw up their hands in disgust and despair. And that's *before* we examine the likes of "education," "entertainment," the booming rush to *legalize drugs* from one end of our country to the other, and the increasing damage they are causing not only to young and impressionable minds, but also to the now greatly tattered fabric of our Republic.

To be sure, the inverse of all of this is that tens of millions of Americans *were overjoyed* with the reelection of President Obama and his desire to greatly expand the All-Government Nanny state. They were overjoyed with the reelection of a man even a far-left reporter for the far-left *New York Times* felt he had to protest by saying the Obama White House was "the greatest enemy of press freedom in a generation" and that any journalist who strayed from the Obama path "would be punished."[3]

3　Fung, Katherine. "New York Times Reporter: Obama Administration Is 'Greatest Enemy Of Press Freedom' In A Generation," Huffington Post, March 2014, http://www.huffingtonpost.com/2014/03/25/james-risen-obama-administration-enemy_n_5027083.html

In case anyone forgets, this criticism is coming from a reporter for a "newspaper" that openly *worships* at the altar of Barack Obama. And yet, there are still tens of millions of Americans out there—the vast majority *incredibly good people*—who question nothing about Obama and accept everything he and his minions utter as gospel. Everything.

As stated before, it is most certainly their right to support such a person. If they want to take pride in a failed president with *zero* real-world experience who had most of what he "earned" handed to him in life, that is their prerogative. Further, if they want to lash themselves to the mast of the ship Mr. Obama built, which is now blasted full of holes by policies solely designed to cripple our economy, health-care system, capitalism, individual freedom, international reputation, national security, and very future, that is also their right.

Just as it is *our* right to feel the need to jump off the ship before it completely sinks and swim to the nearest island where we can establish our own government and live under our rules and our values.

For those millions of other Americans who embrace big government and who did rejoice in the reelection of President Obama, it is my hope this book may serve as a window into the mindset of those who oppose them on purely ideological grounds—fellow Americans who, like them, are *not* the enemy, but simply proud neighbors and even friends who will never be convinced to abandon their core principles.

* * *

On the subject of millions of Americans diametrically opposed to the "values" of millions of *other* Americans, Charles M. Blow, the far-left columnist for the far-left *New York Times* said in part:

> from **"A Nation Divided Against Itself," by Charles M. Blow, the *New York Times*, June 2013**
>
> . . . America is quickly dividing itself into two separate nations, regional enclaves of rigid politics, as the idea of common national priorities fades further into a distant past. . .

To crystallize the growing frustrations of tens of millions of Americans who do believe in Traditional Values and who do recognize the permanent divide as outlined by Mr. Blow and others, below are three headlines that were prominently featured on the must-read, highly-influential *Drudge Report* in reaction to the reelection of Barack Obama as well as to the gridlock that has become our government.

Define "revolution."

Days after that presidential election, eighteen states had petitioned to secede from the United States of America. *Eighteen states.*

Keep in mind that for each state to successfully petition to secede, it has to gather a minimum of twenty-five thousand signatures.

Drudge Report trumpeted the panic and maybe. . . the *beginning of a movement:*

SECESSION MOVEMENT EXPLODES
DRUDGE REPORT
Wednesday, November 14, 2012

The petition of one such state read in part that it chose to secede because:

". . .To withdraw from the union—and to do so—would protect its citizens standard of living and re-secure their rights and liberties in accordance with the original ideas and beliefs of our founding fathers which are no longer being reflected in the federal government."

We petition the Obama administration to:
Peacefully grant the State of Louisiana to withdraw from the United States of America and create its own NEW government.

As the founding fathers of the United States of America made clear in the Declaration of Independence in 1776:

"When in the Course of human events, it becomes necessary for one people to dissolve the political bands which have connected them with another, and to assume among the powers of the earth, the separate and equal station to which the Laws of Nature and of Nature's God entitle them, a decent respect to the opinions of mankind requires that they should declare the causes which impel them to the separation."

". . .Governments are instituted among Men, deriving their just powers from the consent of the governed, that whenever any Form of Government becomes destructive of these ends, it is the Right of the People to alter or abolish it, and institute new Government..."

Created: Nov 07, 2012

After Louisiana petitioned the Obama administration to withdraw from the United States of America, representatives from seventeen other states followed its lead:

18 States Petition To Secede from the U.S.

As of Sunday, November 11, 2012, 18 states have petitioned the Obama Administration for withdrawal from the United States of America in order to "create its own new government". These petitions were created just days after the 2012 presidential election.

Louisiana was the first State to file a petition a day after the election by a Michael E. from Slidell, Louisiana. Texas was the next State to follow by a Micah H. from Arlington, Texas. The government allows one month from the day the petition is submitted to obtain 25,000 signatures in order for the Obama administration to consider the request.

The Texas petition reads as follows:

"The US continues to suffer economic difficulties stemming from the federal government's neglect to reform domestic and foreign spending. The citizens of the US suffer from blatant abuses of their rights such as the NDAA, the TSA, etc.

Given that the state of Texas maintains a balanced budget and is the 15th largest economy in the world, it is practically feasible for Texas to withdraw from the union, and to do so would protect its citizens' standard of living and re-secure their rights and liberties in accordance with the original ideas and beliefs of our founding fathers which are no longer being reflected by the federal government."

While the far-left and the media will not admit it, the number of Americans who believe the way out as highlighted in *Drudge Report* in November of 2012 have grown exponentially since.

CHAPTER 4

IS SECESSION EVEN LEGAL?

The indissoluble link of union between the people of the several states of this confederated nation is, after all, not in the right but in the heart. If the day should ever come (may Heaven avert it!) when the affections of the people of these States shall be alienated from each other; when the fraternal spirit shall give way to cold indifference, or collision of interests shall fester into hatred, the bands of political associations will not long hold together parties no longer attracted by the magnetism of conciliated interests and kindly sympathies; and far better will it be for the people of the disunited states to part in friendship from each other, than to be held together by constraint."

—John Quincy Adams,
on the fiftieth anniversary of the ratification of the Constitution

* * *

As stressed, in support of this critically important and highly controversial project, I felt it imperative to tap into the deep knowledge and massive real-life experience of highly distinguished experts and true patriots.

More than imperative, it was and is the *responsible* action to take.

Across the board, I can't think of anyone more qualified to "war-game" this scenario of Secession than these particular individuals from the "S" Team.

These truly amazing people come from the fields of constitutional law, diplomacy, the military, intelligence, energy, infrastructure, banking, industry, farming, and education. Each and every expert eagerly agreed to contribute information that pertains to precisely his or her expertise.

As of this writing, these individuals have stated they prefer to remain anonymous as they fear that some from the far-left and some from the mainstream media would hunt them down and then target them or their families should their identities become known.

Clearly—as demonstrated by the hacking experience—that's a very valid concern on their part.

That said, *all* agreed to make themselves known to the publisher and editor of this book should the need arise.

* * *

Despite what the far-left may scream and the mainstream media may intimate, those who did voluntarily choose to contribute to this project *are* highly accomplished, highly successful, and about as far removed from a "fringe" character as one can get.

They represent the bedrock of all our Founding Fathers had in mind when they created our nation.

What *does* unite all these experts—based *entirely* on their collective decades of experience in the fields needed to run and protect a nation—is their belief that the United States of America—at least the one they loved—is broken beyond all repair. To a person, they believe that the country of their youth or the nation they fought to preserve and protect while overseas is in terminal freefall with no hope of survival.

They believe it is now a country torn to shreds from its former glorious self by big government zealots, selfish and partisan special interest groups, and the entrenched establishment from both sides looking to take care of themselves at the expense of the American people.

As such it became their strong desire to use *The Secessionist States of America* as the conduit to channel their fears and concerns, and more importantly, their constitutionally and legally permissible *solutions*.

To this point, it should be mentioned that those who served our nation in uniform or in the field of intelligence especially wanted to see this project go forward in protest against those who control most of the "entertainment" world and who continue to vilify, belittle, and dishonor the United States Military and our intelligence services.

It sickens and saddens these patriots to know that almost every time Hollywood produces a movie or television series that is a political or military thriller, invariably, the "evil," "twisted," "greedy," or "traitorous" bad guys turn out to be from the United States Military, the Central Intelligence Agency, or a "fictional" Blackwater-like organization looking to enrich itself while gleefully killing innocent civilians.

These bad guys are *never* the terrorists and Jihadists who plot our extermination 24 hours a day, 365 days a year.

* * *

Ironically, with the continued smearing of our military and intelligence operatives in mind by Hollywood and many liberals—while they continually perform moves a trained contortionist could not pull off to NOT offend Jihadist terrorists—I am reminded of a phone call I had with a very influential agent from one of the most powerful talent agencies in Hollywood.

The conversation took place the *day after* the September 11, 2001, terrorist attacks on New York City and Washington, DC, when the nation was still in complete shock over what had just transpired. I was in my office in Washington, DC, at the time—where traces of smoke could still be seen rising from Pentagon just across the river—with this person calling from the wealth and safety of Beverly Hills.

The conversation is still etched into my mind:

> **ME:** "Hello."
>
> **FAR-LEFT-LIBERAL-AGENT:** (SCREAMING into the phone): "We have to kill all of the Arabs."
>
> **ME:** "Who is this?"
>
> **FLLA:** "WE HAVE TO KILL EVERY ARAB ON THE PLANET!!"
>
> **ME:** "Calm down, please. WHO is this?"
>
> The liberal agent then screamed out a name I instantly recognized before hysterically continuing the tirade.
>
> **FLLA:** "We have to EXTERMINATE them all. We have to start NOW. Today!!"
>
> **ME:** "Please take a few deep breaths and then please listen to yourself. You are Jewish. You are a strong supporter of the State of Israel. Imagine if ten or twenty Israeli settlers who had so twisted their faith to make it pure evil like these terrorists just did, suddenly flew jets into office towers in London, or Paris, or Los

Angeles. What if others from other religions then started screaming that we needed to 'Kill all the Jews.' What would you say to that type of hateful ignorance?"

It was as if this person did not hear one word I had said.

FLLA: "We need to kill every last one of them. We need to KILL all of the ARABS."

ME: "Do you understand that many Arabs are not Muslim? Do you realize that many practice the Christian faith and some are even Jewish? And even for those who do practice the Muslim faith, most will be horrified by what took place yesterday."

FLLA: (Crying now as well as screaming): "KILL THEM. WE NEED TO KILL THEM ALL."

The person then hung up and hopefully soon checked into an insane asylum.

So...we contrast that outright lunacy by a far-left Hollywood agent on September 12, 2001, with the new politically correct insanity emanating out of the Hollywood of today.

In Hollywood, when someone makes a television show or movie so jaw-droppingly bad, they call it "jumping the shark." This term came from the old *Happy Days* sitcom when the writers had long since run out of ideas and decided to have Fonzie jump his motorcycle over a large water tank with a shark swimming inside.

Today, when Hollywood makes a film involving terrorism, they "jump the shark" every single time but don't care, as their theology of political correctness dictates that this be done.

In today's Hollywood, the bad and truly evil guys are almost always white males. Usually white "conservative Christian" males if they can figure out a way to hang those labels around their necks.

Even when it's *not* terrorism, liberal Hollywood is going to make white males the bad guys. A laughable example of this is

Captain America: The Winter Soldier. In a scene where the bad guys dressed as Washington, DC, cops go after the Nick Fury character played by Samuel L. Jackson, all one hundred of them or so are white males. Every single one of them.

A lesser example of this "jumping the shark" political-correctness foolishness are the commercials for home alarm companies. For a number of years, any time these companies do show the "criminals" they are always—and only—white males. Many times, they are white males breaking into the homes of minority couples.

Okay. We get it. White males (except for the liberal ones who run Hollywood, the networks, and the rest of the media) are evil. Especially white Christian males.

So much so that liberal Hollywood has decided that it is the white male who is the true terrorist threatening our (or at least their) way of life.

Why do these liberals *never* portray the Muslim fanatics, who have twisted their faith into true evil, as terrorists?

It is for one main reason: they are scared to death of the repercussions.

As these Hollywood types know (and are counting on), white Christian males will just take the bigoted vilification of themselves in stride. The Muslim fanatics, on the other hand, might decide to track down the Hollywood infidels and behead them.

Yes, liberal Hollywood. Much better to hide under your beds and pretend that this true evil is not advancing toward you, especially as these Jihadists hate you and your "Godlessness" most of all.

* * *

With Hollywood's cowardly, twisted, and eventually suicidal way of thinking serving as just one more motivating factor to this project, now is a good time to ask the question myself and the "S" Team discussed and debated for months:

"Is secession from the United States of America even legal?"

Can this be done?

Here are two quick points on that question before some of the legal arguments in *favor* of secession.

The first is the most basic and the most obvious even if it is forgotten at times: we were all, of course, born "free." If you are an American or individual who does believe in God, then you know that when humans first appeared on the planet, we did so without borders, without governments, and without taxes.

While some might argue that is the most simplistic of statements, the fact of the matter is that it is true.

It is true no matter if you believe that God created us all or you are a liberal "scientist" pushing various far-left agendas who happens to believe the universe and life itself is an accident of the cosmos and that the evolution of humans started when a comet or asteroid smashed into Earth and brought with it the building blocks of life.

No matter which camp you come from—with me being squarely on the side that believes God created the universe and life—there can still be no doubt that humans appeared on the planet government free, tax free, regulation free, and border free.

Governments, regulations, taxes, and borders were created at one time or another by the more powerful and then forced upon the general population of the area.

As that is a reality of humankind, the question then becomes: Can *other* humans force *their* fellow humans to live by *their* rules, in *their* borders, impose unfair taxes, and pay homage to *their* governments, *their* egos, and *their* greed?

The answer of course should be no, but the reality is that *is* the way it has been through recorded time.

Who gave them that authority? *They* gave it to themselves, or took it by force when necessary.

For the tens of millions of Americans who do believe in Traditional Values, there is no doubt they believe strongly in the rule-of-law, safe and secure borders, and a limited government—but…with all those things in service to the *people* and *not* in service to the state, a dictator, or a delusional leader who thinks of himself as a Messiah.

To that exact point and which has been stressed time and again throughout our history: *the Constitution is not an instrument for the government to restrain the people, it is an instrument for the people to restrain the government—lest it come to dominate our lives and interests.*

Well, obviously those who do control, misread, censor, and try to eradicate our Constitution *are* dominating our lives and our interests and have done so for decades now. Knowing that again to be true, we come back to the question of our recent lives:

Is secession from the United States of America even legal?

As far as those behind this project are concerned—again, individuals with a deep respect for, and knowledge of, the words and heroic deeds of our Founding Fathers, the answer is a resounding and unequivocal *yes.*

A large part of the foundation for that unshakeable belief is that we dissolved our bonds from England in 1776 with the Declaration of Independence.

Again, with the Declaration of Independence, our Founding Fathers orchestrated the ultimate act of secession.

Who gave them such liberating authority?

They did.

These men yearned to be free from the ever-tightening shackles of tyranny and decided to take matters into their own hands.

These men risked all—including and especially their very lives—to proclaim:

> We, therefore, the Representatives of the united States of America, in General Congress, Assembled, appealing to the Supreme Judge of the world for the rectitude of our intentions, do, in the Name, and by Authority of the good People of these Colonies, solemnly publish and declare, That these united Colonies are, and of Right ought to be Free and Independent States, that they are Absolved from all Allegiance to the British Crown, and that all political connection between them and the State of Great Britain, is and ought to be totally dissolved; and that as Free and Independent States, they have full Power to levy War, conclude Peace, contract Alliances, establish Commerce, and to do all other Acts and Things which Independent States may of right do. — And for the support of this Declaration, with a firm reliance on the protection of Divine Providence, we mutually pledge to each other our Lives, our Fortunes, and our sacred Honor.

As you read those sacred words, especially note the words: "That these united Colonies are, and of Right ought to be Free and Independent States..."

Simply put, if the federal government—meaning those nationally who control most of our fate—greatly abuses its power in ways that clearly run counter to our Constitution and the intent of our Founding Fathers, then secession from that abusive government becomes the ultimate "check and balance."

* * *

With regard to the subject of secession and its legality, it would be wise—and in fact *mandatory* for all interested in learning more about this particular option—to read the words of the man referred to earlier which were once read by Abraham Lincoln and Robert E. Lee.

Talk about a "time capsule" moment. To know that American statesmen like Lincoln and Lee turned a page and were greeted with the *exact* same words is truly amazing in its historical and constitutional context.

As mentioned earlier, not only was William Rawle a lawyer and appointed as the United States District Attorney of Pennsylvania by George Washington, but he was also acknowledged as one of our greatest constitutional scholars.

In 1829, he wrote *A View of the Constitution of the United States,* a publication that not only became required reading at the United States Military Academy at the time, but that has become one of the seminal documents pertaining to the subject of secession from the Union.

As the *only* purpose of this book is to explore and then present the option for states to be able to legally secede from the United States of America, the essay by William Rawle and the two that follow by Brion McClanahan and Gene H. Kizer, Jr., were chosen with care and should be read in their entirety as they go *directly* to the heart of the matter while making it abundantly clear that *any* state at *any* time most assuredly *does* have the legal and constitutional right to secede from the Union.

Arguments to the contrary—as you will read—are predicated on nonsense, ignorance, complete falsehoods...or dictatorial self-interests.

* * *

First, we have William Rawle's historic and definitive essay on secession and its legality:

from *A View of the Constitution of the United States, Second Edition, 1829*

The Union is an association of the people of republics; its preservation is calculated to depend on the preservation of those republics. The people of each pledge themselves to preserve that form of government in all. Thus each becomes responsible to the rest, that no other form of government shall prevail in it, and all are bound to preserve it in every one.

But the mere compact, without the power to enforce it, would be of little value. Now this power can be nowhere so properly lodged, as in the Union itself. Hence, the term guarantee, indicates that the United States are authorized to oppose, and if possible, prevent every state in the Union from relinquishing the republican form of government, and as auxiliary means, they are expressly authorized and required to employ their force on the application of the constituted authorities of each state, "to repress domestic violence." If a faction should attempt to subvert the government of a state for the purpose of destroying its republican form, the paternal power of the Union could thus be called forth to subdue it.

Yet it is not to be understood, that its interposition would be justifiable, if the people of a state should determine to retire from the Union, whether they adopted another or retained the same form of government, or if they should, with the express intention of seceding, expunge the representative system from their code, and thereby incapacitate themselves from concurring according to the mode now prescribed, in the choice of certain public officers of the United States.

The principle of representation, although certainly the wisest and best, is not essential to the being of a republic, but to continue a member of the Union, it must be preserved, and therefore the guarantee must be so construed. *It depends on the state itself to retain or abolish the principle of representation, because it depends on itself whether it will continue a member of the Union. To deny this right would be inconsistent with the principle on which all our political systems are founded, which is, that the people have in all cases, a right to determine how they will be governed.*

This right must be considered as an ingredient in the original composition of the general government, which, though not expressed, was mutually understood, and the doctrine heretofore presented to the reader in regard to the indefeasible nature of personal allegiance, is so far qualified in respect to allegiance to the United States. It was observed, that it was competent for a state to make a compact with its citizens, that the reciprocal obligations of protection and allegiance might cease on certain events; and it was further observed, that allegiance would necessarily cease on the dissolution of the society to which it was due.

The states, then, may wholly withdraw from the Union, but while they continue, they must retain the character of representative republics. Governments of dissimilar forms and principles cannot long maintain a binding coalition. "Greece," says Montesquieu, "was undone as soon as the king of Macedon obtained a seat in the amphyctionic council." It is probable, however, that the disproportionate force as well as the monarchical form of the new confederate had its share of influence in the event. But whether the historical fact supports the theory or not, the principle in respect to ourselves is unquestionable.

We have associated as republics. Possessing the power to form monarchies, republics were preferred and instituted. The history of the ancient, and the state of the present world, are before us. Of modern republics, Venice, Florence, the United Provinces, Genoa, all but Switzerland have disappeared. They have sunk beneath the power of monarchy, impatient at beholding the existence, of any other form than its own. An injured province of Turkey, recalling to its mind the illustrious deeds of its ancestors, has ventured to resist its oppressors, and with a revival of the name of Greece, a hope is entertained of the permanent institution of another republic. But monarchy stands by with a jealous aspect, and fearful lest its own power should be endangered by the revival of the maxim, that sovereignty can ever reside in the people, affects a cold neutrality, with the probable anticipation that it will induce to barbarian success. Yet that gallant country, it is trusted, will persevere. An enlightened people, disciplined through necessity, and emboldened even by the gloom of its prospects, may accomplish what it would not dare to hope.

This abstract principle, this aversion to the extension of republican freedom, is now invigorated and enforced by an alliance avowedly for the purpose of overpowering all efforts to relieve mankind from their shackles. It is essentially and professedly the exaltation of monarchies over republics, and even over every alteration in the forms of monarchy, tending to acknowledge or secure the rights of the people. The existence of such a combination warrants and requires that in some part of the civilized world, the republican system should be able to defend itself. But this would be imperfectly done, by the erection of separate, independent, though contiguous governments. They must be collected into a body, strong in proportion to the firmness of its union; respected and feared in proportion to its strength. The principle on which alone the Union is rendered valuable, and which alone can continue it, is the preservation of the republican form.

In what manner this guaranty shall be effectuated is not explained, and it presents a question of considerable nicety and importance.

Not a word in the Constitution is intended to be inoperative, and one so significant as the present was not lightly inserted. The United States are therefore bound to carry it into effect whenever the occasion arises, and finding as we do, in the same clause, the engagement to protect each state against domestic violence, which can only be by the arms of the Union, we are assisted in a due construction of the means of enforcing the guaranty. *If the majority of the people of a state deliberately and peaceably resolve to relinquish the republican form of government, they cease to be members of the Union.* If a faction, an inferior number, make such an effort, and endeavour to enforce it by violence, the case provided for will have arisen, and the Union is bound to employ its power to prevent it.

The power and duty of the United States to interfere with the particular concerns of a state are not, however, limited to the violent efforts of a party to alter its constitution. If from any other motives, or under any other pretexts, the internal peace and order of the state are disturbed, and its own powers are insufficient to suppress the commotion, it becomes the duty of its proper government to apply to the Union for protection. This is founded on the sound principle that those in whom the force of the Union is vested, in diminution of the power formerly possessed by the state, are bound to exercise it for the good of the whole, and upon the obvious and direct interest that the whole possesses in the peace and tranquillity of every part. At the same time it is properly provided, in order that such interference may not wantonly or arbitrarily take place; that it shall only be, on the request of the state authorities: *otherwise the self-government of the state might be encroached upon at the pleasure of the Union, and a small state might fear or feel the effects of a combination of larger states against it under colour of constitutional authority;* but it is manifest, that in every part of this excellent system, there has been the utmost care to avoid encroachments on the internal powers of the different states, whenever the general good did not imperiously require it.

No form of application for this assistance is pointed out, nor has been provided by any act of congress, but the natural course would be to apply to the president, or officer for the time being, exercising his functions. No occasional act of the legislature of the United States seems to be necessary, where the duty of the president is pointed out by the Constitution, and great injury might be sustained, if the power was not promptly exercised.

In the instance of foreign invasion, the duty of immediate and unsolicited protection is obvious, but the generic term invasion, which is used without any qualification, may require a broader construction.

If among the improbable events of future times, we shall see a state forgetful of its obligation to refer its controversies with another state to the judicial power of the Union, endeavour by force to redress its real or imaginary wrongs, and actually invade the other state, we shall perceive a case in which the supreme power of the Union may justly interfere; perhaps we may say is bound to do so.

The invaded state, instead of relying merely on its own strength for defence, and instead of gratifying its revenge by retaliation, may prudently call for and gratefully receive the strong arm of the Union to repel the invasion, and reduce the combatants to the equal level of suitors in the high tribunal provided for them. In this course, the political estimation of neither state could receive any degradation. The decision of the controversy would only be regulated by the purest principles of justice, and the party really injured, would be certain of having the decree in its favour carried into effect. It rests with the Union, and not with the states separately or individually, to increase the number of its members. The admission of another state can only take place on its own application. We have already seen, that in the formation of colonies under the denomination of territories, the habit has been, to assure to them their formation into states when the population should become sufficiently large. On that event, the inhabitants acquire a right to assemble and form a constitution for themselves, and the United States are considered as bound to admit the new state into the Union, provided its form of government be that of a representative republic. This is the only check or control possessed by the United States in this respect.

If a measure so improbable should occur in the colony, as the adoption of a monarchical government, it could not be received into the Union, although it assumed the appellation of a state, but the guaranty of which we have spoken, would not literally apply—the guaranty is intended to secure republican institutions to states, and does not in terms extend to colonies. As soon, however, as a state is formed out of a colony, and admitted into the Union, it becomes the common concern to enforce the continuance of the republican form. There can be no doubt, however, that the new state may decline to apply for admission into the Union but it does not seem equally clear, that if its form of government coincided with the rules already mentioned, its admission could be refused. The inhabitants emigrate from the United States, and foreigners are permitted to settle, under the express or implied compact, that when the proper time arrives, they shall become members of the great national community, without being left to an exposed and unassisted independence, or compelled to throw themselves into the arms of a foreign power. It would seem, however, that the constitution adopted, ought to be submitted to the consideration of congress, but it would not be necessary that this measure should take place at the time of its formation, and it would be sufficient if it were presented and approved at the time of its admission. The practice of congress has not, however, corresponded with these positions, no previous approbation of the constitution has been deemed necessary.

It must also be conceded, that the people of the new state retain the same power to alter their constitution, that is enjoyed by the people of the older states, and provided such alterations are not carried so far as to extinguish the republican principle, their admission is not affected.

The secession of a state from the Union depends on the will of the people of such state. The people alone as we have already seen, hold the power to alter their constitution. The Constitution of the United States is to a certain extent, incorporated into the constitutions of the several states by the act of the people. *The state legislatures have only to perform certain organical operations in respect to it.* To withdraw from the Union comes not within the general scope of their delegated authority. There must be an express provision to that effect inserted in the state constitutions. This is not at present the case with any of them, and it would perhaps be impolitic to confide it to them. A matter so momentous, ought not to be entrusted to those who would have it in their power to exercise it lightly and precipitately upon sudden dissatisfaction, or causeless jealousy, perhaps against the interests and the wishes of a majority of their constituents.

But in any manner by which a secession is to take place, *nothing is more certain than that the act should be deliberate, clear, and unequivocal.* The perspicuity and solemnity of the original obligation require correspondent qualities in its dissolution. The powers of the general government cannot be defeated or impaired by an ambiguous or implied secession on the part of the state, although a secession may perhaps be conditional. The people of the state may have some reasons to complain in respect to acts of the general government, they may in such cases invest some of their own officers with the power of negotiation, and may declare an absolute secession in case of their failure. Still, however, the secession must in such case be distinctly and peremptorily declared to take place on that event, and in such case—as in the case of an unconditional secession,—the previous ligament with the Union, would be legitimately and fairly destroyed. But in either case the people is the only moving power.

A suggestion relative to this part of the subject has appeared in print, which the author conceives to require notice.

It has been laid down that if all the states, or a majority of them, refuse to elect senators, the legislative powers of the Union will be suspended.

Of the first of these supposed cases there can be no doubt. If one of the necessary branches of legislation is wholly withdrawn, there can be no further legislation, but if a part, although the greater part of either branch should be withdrawn it would not affect the power of those who remained.

In no part of the Constitution is a specific number of states required for a legislative act. Under the articles of confederation the concurrence of nine states was requisite for many purposes. If five states had withdrawn from that Union, it would have been dissolved. In the present Constitution there is no specification of numbers after the first formation. It was foreseen that there would be a natural tendency to increase the number of states with the increase of population then anticipated and now so fully verified. It was also known, though it was not avowed, that a state might withdraw itself. The number would therefore be variable.

In no part of the Constitution is there a reference to any proportion of the states, except in the two subjects of amendments, and of the choice of president and vice-president.

In the first case, two-thirds or three-fourths of the several states is the language used, and it signifies those proportions of the several states that shall then form the Union.

In the second, there is a remarkable distinction between the choice of president and vice president, in case of an equality of votes for either.

The house of representatives, voting by states, is to select one of the three persons having the highest number, for president, a quorum for this purpose shall consist of a member or members from two-thirds of the states, and a majority of all the states shall be necessary for the choice.

The senate not voting by states, but by their members individually, as in all other cases, selects the vice president from the two persons having the highest number on the list. A quorum for this purpose shall consist of two-thirds of the whole number of senators, and a majority is sufficient for the choice.

Now, if by the omission of the legislators of more than one third of the states, there were no senators from such states, the question would arise whether the quorum is predicated of the states represented, or of all the states, whether represented or not.

The former opinion is most consistent with the general rule, that we should always prefer a construction that will support, to one that has a tendency to destroy an instrument or a system. Other causes than design on the part of a state legislature, may be imagined to occasion some states to be unrepresented in the senate at the moment.

It seems to be the safest, and is possibly the soundest construction, to consider the quorum as intended to be composed of two-thirds of the then existing senators.

But we may pursue the subject somewhat further.

To withdraw from the Union is a solemn, serious act. Whenever it may appear expedient to the people of a state, it must be manifested in a direct and unequivocal manner. If it is ever done indirectly, the people must refuse to elect representatives, as well as to suffer their legislature to re-appoint senators. The senator whose time had not yet expired, must be forbidden to continue in the exercise of his functions.

But without plain, decisive measures of this nature, proceeding from the only legitimate source, the people, the United States cannot consider their legislative powers over such states suspended, nor their executive or judicial powers any way impaired, and they would not be obliged to desist from the collection of revenue within such state.

As to the remaining states among themselves, there is no opening for a doubt.

Secessions may reduce the number to the smallest integer admitting combination. They would remain united under the same principles and regulations among themselves that now apply to the whole. For a state cannot be compelled by other states to withdraw from the Union, and therefore, if two or more determine to remain united, although all the others desert them, nothing can be discovered in the Constitution to prevent it.

The consequences of an absolute secession cannot be mistaken, and they would be serious and afflicting.

The seceding state, whatever might be its relative magnitude, would speedily and distinctly feel the loss of the aid and countenance of the Union. The Union losing a proportion of the national revenue, would be entitled to demand from it a proportion of the national debt. It would be entitled to treat the inhabitants and the commerce of the separated state, as appertaining to a foreign country. In public treaties already made, whether commercial or political, it could claim no participation, while foreign powers would unwillingly calculate, and slowly transfer to it, any portion of the respect and confidence borne towards the United States.

Evils more alarming may readily be perceived. The destruction of the common hand would be unavoidably attended with more serious consequences than the mere disunion of the parts.

Separation would produce jealousies and discord, which in time would ripen into mutual hostilities, and while our country would be weakened by internal war, foreign enemies would be encouraged to invade with the flattering prospect of subduing in detail, those whom, collectively, they would dread to encounter.

Such in ancient times was the fate of Greece, broken into numerous independent republics. Rome, which pursued a contrary policy, and absorbed all her territorial acquisitions in one great body, attained irresistible power.

But it may be objected, that Rome also has fallen. *It is true; and such is the history of man. Natural life and political existence alike give way at the appointed measure of time, and the birth, decay, and extinction of empires only serve to prove the tenuity and illusion of the deepest schemes of the statesman, and the most elaborate theories of the philosopher.* Yet it is always our duty to inquire into, and establish those plans and forms of civil association most conducive to present happiness and long duration: the rest we must leave to Divine Providence, which hitherto has so graciously smiled on the United States of America.

We may contemplate a dissolution of the Union in another light, more disinterested but not less dignified, and consider whether we are not only bound to ourselves but to the world in general, anxiously and faithfully to preserve it.

The first example which has been exhibited of a perfect self-government, successful beyond the warmest hopes of its, authors, ought never to be withdrawn while the means of preserving it remain.

If in other countries, and particularly in Europe, a systematic subversion of the political rights of man shall gradually overpower all rational freedom, and endanger all political happiness, the failure of our example should not be held up as a discouragement to the legitimate opposition of the sufferers; if, on the other hand, an emancipated people should seek a model on which to frame their own structure; our Constitution, as permanent in its duration as it is

> sound and splendid in its principles, should remain to be their guide.
>
> In every aspect therefore which this great subject presents, we feel the deepest impression of a sacred obligation to preserve the union of our country; we feel our glory, our safety, and our happiness, involved in it; we unite the interests of those who coldly calculate advantages with those who glow with what is little short of filial affection; and we must resist the attempt of its own citizens to destroy it, with the same feelings that we should avert the dagger of the parricide.

* * *

After reading this powerful essay from William Rawle, two certainties become abundantly clear:

The first—all things being equal, his overriding hope was that as long as the Union stayed true to the guiding principles of our Constitution and the beliefs of our Founding Fathers, it should remain whole.

The second—*any* state at any time, has the *right* to secede from the Union, especially if her people no longer believe the United States is adhering to the guiding principles of our Constitution or the vision of our Founding Fathers.

In such a case, to quote Mr. Rawle, "nothing is more certain than that the act should be deliberate, clear, and unequivocal."

While the subject terrifies some, the absolute constitutional reality is that states *do* have the right to secede from the Union. *Period.*

To accomplish the task, an individual state legislature need only to vote in favor of secession and sign a declaration—much like the Declaration of Independence—proclaiming such. Once this is complete, that particular state would be an independent country.

* * *

Staying on topic with the question of the legality of secessionism we have the following excerpts from an exceptional essay by Dr. Brion McClanahan, who is not only a highly respected and trusted historian, but also a bestselling author.

Said Mr. McClanahan in part:

from "Is Secession Legal?" TheAmericanConservative.com, December 2012

With all fifty states offering petitions to the central government to leave the Union, the legality of secession is now front page news in the United States. Can a state legally secede from the Union? Many, including Supreme Court justice Antonin Scalia, suggest no. In a 2006 letter, Scalia argued that a the question was not in the realm of legal possibility because 1) the United States would not be party to a lawsuit on the issue 2) the "constitutional" basis of secession had been "resolved by the Civil War," and 3) there is no right to secede, as the Pledge of Allegiance clearly illustrates through the line "one nation, indivisible."

. . . These arguments seem like a fairly strong case against secession. Three Supreme Court justices, one famous president, a bloody war, and the language of a modern pledge of allegiance offer conclusive proof that secession, while an entertaining philosophical exercise, has no legal basis. *Their various opinions and conclusions, however, all have gaping holes.*

Scalia's positions are the most vapid. Secession, as accomplished by the Southern states in 1860 and 1861 and as discussed by the North at the Hartford Convention in 1815, is an independent act by the people of the states, and accomplished in the same fashion as the several conventions that occurred throughout early American history. The United States would never be a party to a lawsuit on the issue because secession, both *de facto* and *de jure,* is an extra-legal act of self-determination, *and once the States have seceded from the Union, the Constitution is no longer in force in regard to the seceded political body. This same rule applies to the Article I, Section 10 argument against secession. If the Constitution is no longer in force—the States have separated and resumed their independent status—then the Supreme Court would not have jurisdiction and therefore could not determine the "legality" of the move.*

The Union, then, through a declaration of war could attempt to force the seceded States to remain, but even if victorious that would not solve a philosophical issue. *War and violence do not and cannot crush the natural right of self-determination.* It can muddle the picture and force the vanquished into submission so long as the boot is firmly planted on their collective throats, but a bloody nose and a prostrate people settles nothing. Oliver Ellsworth of Connecticut said in 1788 that he feared a "coercion of arms" in relation to a delinquent state. "This Constitution does not attempt to coerce sovereign bodies, states, in their political capacity. No coercion is applicable to such bodies, but that of an armed force. If we should attempt to execute the laws of the Union by sending an armed force against a delinquent state, it would involve the good and the bad, the innocent and the guilty, in the same calamity." Ellsworth recognized, as did the majority of the founding generation, that force did not destroy sovereignty. It created artificial supremacy, but sovereignty, the basic tenant of the founding, could not be surrendered in such a manner. Sovereignty, in fact, cannot be surrendered at all; it can be delegated, as in the powers granted to the general government in Article I, but never surrendered.

His "Pledge of Allegiance" analogy is the most absurd argument of the bunch. The modern pledge was written by Francis Bellamy, *a socialist minister* who wanted to indoctrinate American schoolchildren with a nationalist message, one based on the "great speeches" of Daniel Webster and Abraham Lincoln in relation to the "One Nation which the Civil War was fought to prove." Sprinkle in some "liberty and justice" from the French Revolution and you have a message that any good leftist nationalist can embrace. The founding generation would not have said such a pledge, if for no other reason that most did not view the United States as a "nation" in the strict sense of the word, a single people.

The other issues involved in the debate are slightly more complicated, but in several instances come back to Scalia's more simplistic analysis. In the *Texas v. White* decision, Chase implicitly reasoned that the Union was an "indissoluble" contract between the "American people" and the federal government, or in this case the people of Texas and the federal government. All contracts are intended to be perpetual. But if this were the case, how could nine States ratify a new Constitution while four States remained part of another Union in clear violation of the language of the Articles of Confederation. Changes to the Articles required the consent of all thirteen States, not nine, and thus the Constitution can be viewed, in part, as an act of secession.

Moreover, James Madison argued that the Union was a different type of contract. "We are not to consider the Federal Union as analogous to the social compact of individuals: for if it were so, a majority would have a right to bind the rest, and even to form a new constitution for the whole...." The Constitution was framed by the unanimous consent of the States present in convention assembled in Philadelphia, but it had no teeth until the States, in convention, ratified it. Even at that point, Madison suggested, the States could not bind the rest into accepting the document or remaining in the Union. The Constitution does not have a coercive principle, as Ellsworth called it. An "indissoluble" Union would suggest that it does.

Waging war "against them (the States)" is an act of treason, and as per the Constitution, a State can only be "protected" by the central government on the application of the legislature or the executive in the case of invasion. Lincoln violated both constitutional safeguards against coercion by the central government in 1861, of course only if the states remained in the Union, as he insisted they did. If not, war required a declaration from Congress, something Lincoln did not have, and by declaring war, Congress would have recognized the Confederate States as a legitimate government. Either way, Lincoln violated the Constitution, thus rendering the "bloody nose" argument against secession void.

The "one people" argument was dissected by John Taylor of Caroline and Abel P. Upshur in their respective commentaries on the document. In his *New Views of the Constitution of the United States*, Taylor contended that the continuity between the Articles of Confederation and the Constitution reinforced the sovereignty of the states, and declared that, "There are many states in America, but no state of America, nor any people of an American state. A constitution for America or Americans, would therefore have been similar to a constitution for Utopia or Utopians." This view is in sharp contrast to Chase, who argued that continuity maintained a "perpetual" Union. Taylor wrote, "This construction bestows the same meaning upon the same words in our three constituent or elemental instruments, and exhibits the reason why the whole language of the constitution is affianced to the idea of a league between sovereign states, and hostile to that of a consolidated nation."

Upshur was more direct in his defense of both nullification and secession as a right of the sovereign States. Published as a direct attack on Story's polemic, Upshur's *A Brief Enquiry into the True Nature and Character of Our Federal Government* is perhaps the last great commentary of the antebellum period. Upshur decried the "imaginative construction" of people like Story and Webster and insisted that consolidation was never the aim of the Constitution. In defending the right so the States to control the government and "interpose" their sovereignty to curtail central authority, Upshur said:

The checking and controlling influences which afford safety to public liberty, are not to be found in the government itself. The people cannot always protect themselves against their rulers; if they could, no free government, in past times, would have been overthrown. Power and patronage cannot easily be so limited and defined, as to rob them of their corrupting influences over the public mind. It is truly and wisely remarked by the Federalist, that "a power over a man's subsistence is a power over his will." As little as possible of this power should be entrusted to the federal government, and even that little should be watched by a power authorized and competent to arrest its abuses. That power can be found only in the states. In this consists the great superiority of the federative system over every other. In that system, the federal government is responsible, not directly to the people *en masse*, but to the people in their character of distinct political corporations. However easy it may be to steal power from the people, governments do not so readily yield it to one another. The confederated states confer on their common government only such power as they themselves cannot separately exercise, or such as can be better exercised by that government. They have, therefore, an equal interest, to give it power enough, and to prevent it from assuming too much. In their hands the power of interposition is attended with no danger; it may be safely lodged where there is no interest to abuse it.

During the Philadelphia Convention of 1787, Gouverneur Morris of Pennsylvania outlined "the distinction between a federal and a national supreme government; the former being a mere compact resting on the good faith of the parties, the latter having a complete and compulsive operation." If the Constitution established a federal government, and it did, then the Constitution did not have a "compulsive operation." In essence, the people of the states in convention could either interpose their sovereignty to arrest the acts of the general government or withdraw from the Union. Morris, a nationalist, recognized that the states still held sway when he suggested that the Constitution be voted on by state and that the states, not a consolidated people, had to ratify the document. The Constitution as ratified in 1787 and 1788 is "a mere compact resting on the good faith of the parties." That compact can be unilaterally broken at any point by the same people of the States which ratified it.

Neither the Framers nor the ratifiers believed that the Constitution created a "consolidated nation" as Story suggested. It was argued in all state ratifying conventions that the opposite was true. The Union was made "more perfect" but never consolidated. The States still had all powers not delegated to the general government, as the Tenth Amendment to the Constitution clearly illustrates, and every State proposed a "Tenth Amendment" in their suggested bill of rights in the months after ratification. John C. Calhoun wrote that, "I maintain that sovereignty is in its nature indivisible. It is the supreme power in a state, and we might just as well speak of half a square, or half a triangle, as of half a sovereignty." In other words, delegated powers were still retained by the people of the States at large for their exercise if they chose to rescind that delegation. *Sovereignty can never be divided or surrendered in part. If the states had it in 1776 as Jefferson wrote, then they maintain that sovereignty to this day and thus can exercise that sovereignty through an act of interposition or withdraw.*

As for those who suggest that a state carved from the common property of the United States does not have the same sovereignty as the original thirteen states, *Jefferson made clear in his Northwest Ordinance of 1787 that new states would enter the Union on "equal footing" with the existing states, meaning that they had the same rights, privileges, and immunities as the original thirteen, including the right of interposition and withdrawal.* Jefferson himself authored the Kentucky Resolutions of 1798, a clear indication that he believed as much. Kentucky was not one of the original states, but the people of Kentucky had the same right of recourse that the people of Virginia had in opposing the unconstitutional Sedition Act of 1798. If the argument against this position is correct, then the original thirteen states, themselves pared from the territory of Great Britain, would be illegal and illegitimate. That is not the case.

Secession and interposition—nullification—are healthy discussions to have in a federal republic. There mere threat can, and has, spurred the central government to reform... Secession is a manifestation of the fear that the situation will not improve. Perhaps that is the case, but Dickinson faced the same situation in the 1770s.

Often called the "Penman of the Revolution" for his famous *Letters from a Farmer in Pennsylvania,* Dickinson understood that a final break with the crown may occur, but he urged his fellow colonists to be cautious... but if conventions are called, and they must be at this point, all options should be on the table. That would be the Dickinsonian solution to the problem. "Experience," he said in 1787, "must be our only guide. Reason may mislead us."[4]

---

4 Used with permission from Dr. Brion McClanahan.

* * *

To close out this chapter, we have even more emphatic words upholding the legality of secession as presented by Gene H. Kizer, Jr., from a convincing essay he authored:

> **from "The Right of Secession," BonnieBluePublishing.com**
>
> There is no evidence that secession was illegal or prohibited by the Constitution, and in fact there is almost overwhelming evidence to the contrary, that secession was a legal, constitutionally sanctioned act... There had to be a specific constitutional prohibition on secession for it to be illegal... The arguments for the right of secession are unequivocal. There is the constitutional right based on the Compact Theory, and the revolutionary right based on the idea that a free people have the right to change their government anytime they see fit.

Mr. Kizer then closes his piece with a factual observation—as mentioned earlier when discussing the American Civil War—that many far-left "historians" and "educators" choose to ignore, deny, or reinvent.

That factual observation follows:

> The Southern states did not rush headlong into secession. They had enormous grievances against the North that were much greater than even Northern violations of the

Constitution... They did so peacefully and with great intellectual vigor and in the end, the people of the South struck for independence and self-government, just as their fathers in the Revolution had.

Amen to all, Mr. Kizer. Especially those last words regarding the South, the Civil War, and secession.

CHAPTER 5

HOW WOULD WE SECEDE?

Well...like the eleven southern states who—*peacefully*—seceded from the Union in 1860 and 1861, the departing state would simply hold a convention, signal its intent, and leave.

As the first state to so secede before the Civil War—for reasons just outlined—South Carolina offered up the following declaration:

We, the people of the State of South Carolina, in convention assembled, do declare and ordain, and it is hereby declared and ordained, That the ordinance adopted by us in convention on the twenty-third day of May, in the year of our Lord one thousand seven hundred and eighty-eight, whereby the Constitution of the United States of America was ratified, and also all acts and parts of acts of the General Assembly of this State ratifying amendments of the said Constitution, are hereby repealed; and that the union now subsisting between South Carolina and other States, under the name of the "United States of America," is hereby dissolved.

—Done at Charleston the twentieth day of December, in the year of our Lord one thousand eight hundred and sixty.

It must be stressed and recognized that because Abraham Lincoln did not become president until March 1861, James Buchanan was still president when the first southern states seceded from the Union. While President Buchanan expressed his strong disagreement with such a move, he decided that using the Union Army against these states would be *unconstitutional.*

Unfortunately for the 750,000 killed from both sides, Abraham Lincoln either did not agree with President Buchanan or *purposely* violated the Constitution to "preserve the Union."

Now, nearly two centuries after William Rawle's thoughts on the subject, if the people of a state or states *were* inclined to secede from the United States of America in such a way that "the act should be deliberate, clear, and unequivocal," then author, writer, and historian Russell D. Longcore offers up an excellent example of why it would be entirely and constitutionally legal and *how* it could possibly come about in his own thought-provoking essay written to start or continue the dialogue many of us are now having:

from **"Here Is How To Secede From The Union,"**
DumpDC.wordpress.com, 2012

You may think that this article is too simplistic, and omits important issues...I submit that if secession is not made so simple that a child can understand it, it will not happen in your state. Its logic has to be made so unassailable that only a fool would resist it.

How To Secede From The United States of America:
1. Philosophy

Each individual must come to his or her own conclusion that secession is the only way to regain liberty, and each state must make its secession decision independent of any other state.

2. Initiation

Secession should be solemnly deliberated by the elected representatives and the state citizens. Secession should be initiated at the moment that any state reaches the point at which it will no longer accept the despotic tyranny and laws coming from the US Federal Government in Washington, DC. Or, secession should be initiated upon a collapse of the Dollar, or the imposition by Washington DC of martial law in the event of social upheaval.

There is no written, formal method for initiating and completing an act of secession. If history can be our guide, we see that the states of 1860 completed their secessions by specially-elected conventions or by referendum. But the secession could also be initiated by a Governor and the State Legislature in assembly.

It would be excellent if a seated Governor would lead his state into secession. The easiest way for a state to secede would be for the State Legislature, either unicameral or bicameral, to draft a Declaration of Secession document and an Ordinance of Secession document. Then the Legislature should take a roll call vote and pass a Joint Resolution of Secession in legislature assembled, and have the Governor sign the Resolution instantly upon its passage. This process should be done on live TV, with all proceedings televised and recorded.

Allowing the world to view this process in non-edited real time would be one of the most exciting and historic TV broadcasts ever made. The eyes of the world would be fixed on the TV feed and little else would be reported or discussed on its programming. Hell, run commercials and make some money for the state. Why should the networks get this historic event for free?

If the Legislature and Governor refused to support secession, a petition initiative could garner enough signatures of registered voters to force a referendum. Each state has statutes about petition initiatives for referenda. The Texas Nationalist Movement is doing a petition initiative right now, with the intent of presenting the petitions to the Legislature on day one of the 2011 legislative session. Follow the law in your state.

If there was a statewide referendum on secession it could be a simply worded ballot question like: "Shall the citizens of the State of XXXX repeal the 1788 ratification of the Constitution of the United States of America by the State of XXXX, and shall the citizens of the State of XXXX resume all the rights and powers granted under said Constitution?" A simple "Yes" or "No" vote will suffice.

If that's too flowery for you, here's an even simpler question: "Shall the citizens of the State of XXXX secede from the United States of America?" A "Yes" or "No" vote will suffice.

A simple majority of votes would pass the referendum.

The referendum should only be done with paper ballots that will be counted by hand, no machines, no electronic voting. Further, the referendum should not be scheduled for only one single day, but over at least three days, preferably a weekend...to facilitate the greatest possible participation by registered voters. Finally, a photo ID should be required as verification of identity for eligibility to vote. This ain't the American way of widespread voter fraud...this is the state's rights secession way. It's also my article, and I can write the rules any way I choose.

Another method of moving secession along in your state might be to organize on a county-by-county basis. The County Commission could either call for a countywide referendum on the question of secession, or could nominate a delegate to participate in a Secession Convention.

3. Secession Convention

Each state's Secession Convention, formed to contemplate, design and complete the process of secession, should draft a Declaration of Secession.

Many of the seceding states of 1860 wrote and ratified a Declaration of Secession, also known as a "Declaration of Causes." Each Declaration enumerated that particular state's reasons for secession, in like manner to the 1776 Declaration of Independence sent to King George by the Colonists.

Once the Declaration of Secession is prepared, the Chair of the Secession Convention or the Governor should deliver signed original copies of the document to the President of the United States, the Speaker of the

US House of Representatives, and the President of the Senate (televised live of course).

4. Ordinance of Secession.

Then the seceding states must prepare an Ordinance of Secession. Here below is the simple, succinct wording of the South Carolina Ordinance of Secession of 1860:

AN ORDINANCE to dissolve the union between the State of South Carolina and other States united with her under the compact entitled "The Constitution of the United States of America."

We, the people of the State of South Carolina, in convention assembled do declare and ordain, and it is hereby declared and ordained, That the ordinance adopted by us in convention on the twenty-third day of May, in the year of our Lord one thousand seven hundred and eighty-eight, whereby the Constitution of the United States of America was ratified, and also all acts and parts of acts of the General Assembly of this State ratifying amendments of the said Constitution, are hereby repealed; and that the union now subsisting between South Carolina and other States, under the name of the "United States of America," is hereby dissolved.

Done at Charleston the twentieth day of December, in the year of our Lord one thousand eight hundred and sixty.

That is the sum total of all the words necessary to complete the secession.

Once the Ordinance of Secession is prepared (televised live), the Chair of the Secession Convention or the Governor should deliver signed original copies of the document to the President of the United States, the Speaker of the US House of Representatives, and the President of the Senate (also televised live).

That is the process of secession from the United States of America. That was the easy part. Then the REAL WORK begins.

The first thing the new sovereign state should do is to form a Constitutional Convention, and create a new government.

Question: What if Washington files a Federal lawsuit or injunction in Federal Court to stop the state from seceding?

Answer: Once the state formally secedes, it is no longer subject to US Federal Court jurisdiction, is it? Is it not a sovereign nation after secession, just like any other nation of the world? So, the seceding state could answer any legal maneuver by rejecting the jurisdiction of the US Federal Courts. Remember, Washington doesn't OWN your state. Washington was formed by the states to be an errand-boy for the states. Who runs who?

Question: What if Washington invades our state with military forces?

Answer: That is the reason that your state needs a well-trained state militia.

Question: What will we do for money?

Answer: The state must make gold and silver the only legal tender.

Isn't the process of secession much like writing this short note to end a relationship?

Dear Washington: It's over. We're leaving. We ain't asking your permission to leave. We ain't asking for a legal divorce. We're just ending this relationship right here and now. We're rescinding the authority we gave you in 1788. Leave us alone. Goodbye.

In conclusion, try to envision yourself and your family in a new nation created by secession. All the people you meet are excited and breathless in their anticipation of the future. The general opinion of the populace is pure unbridled optimism. The new nation's economy is booming, the money is backed by gold and silver, and there is no inflation. "Now Hiring" signs are in all the shop windows. The newspaper's "Help Wanted" ads are packed full. Prices for goods and services are low, and the stores are loaded with goods. Manufacturers are streaming into the new nation to take advantage of the rare pro-business atmosphere. Wages are climbing steadily in manufacturing jobs as companies compete for the best and brightest for their employees. New businesses are being created at a fever pace. Residential and commercial construction is at a high level to meet the demand of the new residents.

All because one state recognized this historic opportunity and realized the dream of liberty through the process of state secession.

Secession is the hope for humanity. *Who will be first?*[5]

---

5 Used with permission from Russell D. Longcore.

Well, Russell. In answer to your heartfelt and patriotic closing question: more and more Americans are lining up to be first.

* * *

To be sure, the United States of America—even as flawed and as failing as it clearly is—is still *the* best model on Earth with regard to how to change governments in the most peaceful, legal, and orderly way possible.

No matter how contentious or controversial the election— George W. Bush versus Al Gore in 2000 being a prime example— the transition that takes place at noon on January 20 every four years is still a highly laudable civics lesson in motion.

It is truly a thing of beauty that sets our nation apart and above so many others.

That, of course, is the good news. As far as transitions go, peaceful and admirable is nice, but if, at the end of the day—or the beginning of the year after the November election in this case—we are transitioning from *one corrupt political party* to *another corrupt political party*, then it really does not matter how peaceful or orderly the transition may be.

Switching out one defective part for another defective part is the height of lunacy and yet, we continue to practice that particular brand of insanity every two, four, and six years.

Unfortunately, over the last number of presidential and election cycles, the product has gone from bad to worse as both sides not only slid deeper into the cesspool of the entrenched establishment, but gleefully looked after only themselves while willfully disregarding the welfare of their confused, scared, and *completely leaderless* constituents.

As the Democrat and Republican parties have proven, while you still can't beat something with nothing, you can continually beat *nothing* with *nothing*.

But as we have learned in the most painful and regressive ways possible, when nothing beats and then *succeeds* nothing, it is *always* the people who suffer.

Now, while all people *are* created equal, not all people are created equal when it comes to how they *react* to adversity, corruption, criminal conduct, or the seeming permanence of a government run by incompetent politicians who put themselves and their parties before all.

When all avenues of reason and hope are exhausted, a tiny percentage of the people ultimately *will* eventually break free from the herd, stand their ground, and fight.

They will fight for their very survival and the survival of their children.

Well, as we have all witnessed, "reason" caught the last stagecoach out of Dodge a long time ago. It's as over as over is going to get.

As I asked at the beginning of this book: If not us, who? If not now, when?

For our purposes as well as for historical precedent—and as highlighted at the beginning—Thomas Jefferson and our other Founding Fathers knew exactly when the time had come and boldly decided the "now" and the "who." They felt they not only had no choice, but that, as Patriots in a position to *do something*, it was their *responsibility* to act. And act they did.

Once again, as precisely spelled out to us by our Founding Fathers in the Declaration of Independence:

When, in the course of human events, it becomes necessary for one people to dissolve the political bands which have connected them with another, and to assume among the powers of the earth the separate and equal station to which the Laws of Nature and of Nature's God entitle them, a decent respect to the opinions of mankind requires that they should declare the causes which impel them to separation . . . Governments are instituted among Men, deriving their just powers from the consent of the governed, that whenever any Form of Government becomes destructive of these ends, *it is the Right of the People to alter—or—abolish it, and institute new Government...*

While the wise and needed advice of Thomas Jefferson and our Founding Fathers was relevant and of critical importance—both then and now—the fact of the matter is we don't want to "alter" or "abolish" anything. We just want to *leave.*

We want to—and in fact, *need to*—leave the All-Government Nanny state Traveling Freak Show as far behind as soon as possible.

More than anyone, the advisors to this project know that, believe it, and should the *theoretical* someday become reality, understand that they—like Thomas Jefferson—have a responsibility to help *lead* the exodus.

That said, this book and this concept is *not* about a revolution— at least not a "revolution" in the traditional sense of the word. As diagramed, this revolution will be peaceful and will be a revolution like no other in history. It will be a revolution by . . . *migration.*

Our team of advisors—including the special operations operatives who have served us all so valiantly overseas—have given this component of the project their full and undivided attention and respect for the obvious reason. It means *everything.*

This strategy would be *the* strategy. Without this strategy, there is no peaceful, legal, and entirely constitutional secession. Without this strategy, there is *no* hope of a new nation.

Without this strategy, there is no hope...period.

Fortunately, we do have this team of advisors, we do have their strategies, and we do have their blueprint so...we do have hope.

The brilliance of this strategy is in its simplicity.

With the territory of our new Republic *now* identified, the advisors then turned their attention to the legal and constitutional steps that would have to be taken to have those states secede from the United States of America.

Not only would they need the will of the people, but they also would have to deal with the corrupt and pervasive entrenched establishment. How best to win over that corrupt entrenched establishment and have them side with secession?

Obviously, the short answer is you can't win them over. Ever. At least not in a legal and ethical way. As one of these corrupt politicians once infamously said: "My vote can't be bought—however, it can be rented."

So, short of bribery, blackmail, or intimidation, how best to change the odds in our favor?

Simple. *Get rid* of the corrupt entrenched establishment. Make them and their institutional corruption completely irrelevant to the cause.

The best way to get rid of them is to vote them out of office and out of power. The best way to do *that* is to change the entire dynamic of the states that will form our new Republic.

How?

By changing and shifting the *collective population* of those states. In other words, by salting the mines. *Salt* the states with Traditional Values voters.

What started out as an off-the-wall comment about "taking over Australia" soon evolved into a real discussion point. From there, the complete team of advisors to this project started to "run the numbers" on an idea originally said in jest. The more they did the math, the more it made complete sense.

For us, a country created by getting enough like-minded Americans to move to new states which would then transition into a new Republic quickly became a very viable and legitimate strategy. A strategy that had the safety and interests of the people at its core. *All* the people.

"Is this really possible?" team members kept asking each other.

The more questions asked and the more answers given, the more they knew they possessed the passion, the power, and the will to *make* it happen.

As the pros and the cons of the project were honestly debated and dissected, it became clearer that the pros heavily outweighed the cons.

This could actually be done. We *could* and *should* follow the lead of South Carolina in December of 1860.

The more we crunched the numbers, the more certain we grew that this "revolution by migration" could succeed with a relatively minute percentage of the population involved.

There was and is a way to tip the scale *back to our favor*, at least enough to effect the change we are seeking.

For our team of advisors, this would mean spreading the word far and wide—within these states and without—that a new nation is about to be built and established upon the rock-solid foundation of those Traditional Values.

To spread the word, of course, the true believers in this dream of a new nation—you, me, the "S" Team—would be on their own. The mainstream media—who are now nothing more than propagandists for the far-left—would do *everything in their power* to squelch the story of the movement and especially the rationale for taking this history-making step.

No problem. The patriots behind this movement would simply circumvent them and get the word out through alternative media, talk radio, and the leading conservative, libertarian, and independent sites. Within a *few days at most,* the word would go forth from one corner of the United States to the other:

> A new nation is being created true to the words and deeds of our Founding Fathers and built upon the foundation of strict Traditional Values. All Americans who share these values and wish to free themselves and their children from the chains of socialist doctrine are encouraged to make their way when ready to this new nation and become citizens of the only nation on Earth dedicated to liberty in its purest sense.

Our advisors would then repeat that message again and again as they continually encouraged any and all Americans who shared their values to relocate themselves and their families to the states now making up our Republic.

Easy? Far from it. It would—and will—be the most difficult project in the lives of all involved. For more on the difficult reality of this mission, see chapter 8: A New Continental Congress.

While far from easy, based upon their own research and experience, our advisors are still confident that, if their blueprint is put into action, ultimately millions of Americans would begin the most *historic migration* of people the world has ever known since Moses led the "chosen people" to the Promised Land.

As this migration of faith, values, and patriotism gained momentum and national and international attention, and became unstoppable, most liberals, or just ordinary people living in the territory chosen to be our new Republic, would most certainly choose to move *out* of those states.

There is not only nothing wrong with that decision, but it is also their right as American citizens. At least it is from *our* perspective as individuals who still respect the rule-of-law.

More on this later as well, but that outcome is also *part* of the blueprint drawn up by our advisors to take this new nation from the theoretical to the *actual*. Those openly opposed to our new nation and its values—for whatever reasons—would also most certainly vote against secession once the day comes.

As far as our advisors are concerned, it's much better these individuals know the outcome of that vote is a fate accompli. Better to have them quickly come to the realization that as far as their far-left All-Government theology is concerned, all *is* lost. There may be *other places* to practice their worship of an all-controlling government, but it would *not* be in our new Republic and *never* will be again.

For our advisors and all of us who agree with them, this long-awaited moment in time will be *our* declaration—our Declaration of Independence and freedom from the oppressive and suicidal tenets of the All-Government Nanny state.

We will make *no apologies for our beliefs* nor the *actions taken* to secure our rights as a free people.

That said, we would *honestly extend* our strong belief in freedom to those who disagree with our movement or even actively oppose us. We *deeply respect* their right to dissent. Those living in the territory chosen to be our new Republic who choose to leave will be given and afforded every consideration and courtesy.

Of course, as stated, many will choose to leave. As must be stressed again, our advisors do estimate that by the hundreds of thousands—liberals, those abusing the public-employee pensions, many from the mainstream media, many teachers and professors trying to indoctrinate our young people into worshiping at the altar of the All-Government Nanny state, and all those opposed to the movement for a variety of reasons—will eventually flee this new Republic and transition back to the *land of unfunded entitlements, something for nothing, no accountability, no rule of law, politically correct favored religion, open borders, immoral entertainment, legalized discrimination, and massive political corruption.*

Again, this liberal and far-left migration *out* of our new nation is all part of the plan.

It *has* to happen.

These hundreds of thousands of "non-believers" will be replaced by Americans desperate to immerse themselves in the cocoon of faith, security, and Traditional Values who will flood *into* this new Republic.

With these millions of patriots will come literally *hundreds of billions* in treasure. "Treasure" in terms of money, talent, experience, faith, certitude, and *resolve.* That is the secret of success here. That is the "ace in the hole" for our new nation. The "treasure" of *our people* will eclipse any known treasure on Earth as ours will be a *treasure of faith, values, and hope.*

It will be a treasure that *will* fund and sustain our new nation for decades to come.

CHAPTER 6

THE NEW REPUBLIC: WHERE WILL IT BE SITUATED?

With *serious* people giving *serious* thought to this project came a very serious question to be answered by the greater team: *where* would this new Republic be situated?

It doesn't get any easier after answering that question. Hot on its heels are: When would this new nation be created? How large will this new nation be? How will it be populated? How will it sustain itself? And, most important of all, if the previous questions are solved: How would this new nation *defend itself* if needed?

To each and every question, the individuals who make up the "S" Team brought his and her own thoughts and expertise to the table as they often struggled with the answers to these necessary but difficult and highly charged questions.

As such, what started off as more or less an interesting *academic* exercise a few years prior has now understandably morphed into a *passion* as these patriots scramble to articulate their vision for this new nation while time is still on their side and they are still free to speak their minds and exercise their First Amendment rights.

Make no mistake, these highly accomplished men and women not only believe time is running out, but also that the Nanny state, All-Government intelligentsia that currently runs most of our nation is quickly putting the final pieces of the totalitarian puzzle in place to intimidate—or even silence—*all* dissenting opinion.

Believing this to be the case, it became imperative to finish this project so as to at least have a rudimentary blueprint in place that would reestablish a path to liberty and Traditional Values for the millions of Americans who share the "S" Team's growing concern for the fate of our Republic.

For myself and these advisors, freedom is no longer on the march, but instead quickly *receding* as it is being *hunted down* across the country and across the globe in the name of Socialism-on-steroids as crafted and implemented by the wealthy and privileged far-left elite. As we know all too well, freedom is not only being threatened by fanatical terrorism and the forces of evil around the globe, but shockingly from "progressive" zealots *within* the United States.

Which group *honestly* represents the *greatest threat* to our liberty and well-being?

With *that* question echoing in our minds, we circle back to the first question of the hour:

Where exactly will this new nation be located?

In every *single* state within the United States of America are citizens desperate to free themselves and their families from this increasing and seemingly unstoppable threat to their liberty and welfare.

Tens of millions of Americans.

And yet, not every state can be folded into the new Republic.

In actuality, only *three states*—at least at the onset—would be designated as the landmass from which our new Republic would rise.

Only three states out of fifty.

But individuals from all fifty states who want to live in the country of their hopes and dreams would be welcome in these three states, the land from which would be transformed into a historic new nation.

More than welcomed, they would *be* the new Republic and represent its very conscience.

After some spirited debate, a unanimous consensus was reached quickly among this august group of advisors.

Because of the *unique set of criterion* needed to form this new nation, most of the landmass of the United States of America was immediately eliminated from consideration. Again, not because hundreds of thousands of people in those states did not fit the ideological template being used to identify those who would be honored and anxious to live in this new Republic, but rather because the logistics or political circumstances of their home states did not meet the high standards needed to give a fledgling nation a realistic chance of survival.

As regions and states were crossed off the list of potential candidates, it quickly became evident which region of the country and which states within that region were elevating themselves above the others as far as the logistical and political needs were concerned.

Much sooner than anyone on the "S" Team had anticipated, the landmass was identified where our "theoretical" new Republic would be brought to life: circled in bright red on a large map of the United States of America were the states of *South Carolina, Georgia,* and *Florida.*

Three states giving hope to a better life.

Three states that could become "one nation under God."

Why those states?

What did they have which the other forty-seven did not?

First, as obvious to all who deeply believe in Traditional Values and have a clear understanding of the insurmountable issues plaguing our nation, many states in the Northeast, the North, and the West would not be suitable for a host of reasons, not the least of which being their own eager embrace of the All-Government Nanny state mentality.

Beyond that obvious disqualification, it still came down to a matter of logistics.

Which area would afford the new nation the very best chance at survival?

Time and again as the "S" Team poured over the data, the states of *South Carolina, Georgia,* and *Florida* jumped out at them.

WHY WERE SOUTH CAROLINA, GEORGIA, AND FLORIDA CHOSEN?

There are a number of critically important reasons why those three states were chosen, but what follows are the reasons at the top of the *wish list.*

All three states are not only incredibly rich in natural resources, but also border the Atlantic Ocean and the Gulf of Mexico and would—among many other positives—be able to exercise their *inalienable rights to drill for oil and natural gas within their borders and off their shores* and thereby eventually bring *hundreds of billions* of dollars of added revenue into this new Republic.

This right would be crucially important for the new Republic.

The three states combined have a coastline of about 1,500 miles. That's 1,500 miles with direct access to two critical bodies of water. For years, the United States and much of the world have been held hostage to oil being supplied by rogue or even terrorist nations. Shockingly, we have been held hostage to this reality even though we have *billions of barrels* of oil right off our own coastline or beneath the southwest section of Florida. Enough oil, in fact, to not only free us from the extortion of these terrorist states, but also allow us to become one of the largest *exporters* of oil in the world.

Why haven't we taken advantage of this generous and life-sustaining reality?

Because many from the far-left who hope to "green" the United States at the direct expense of our economy and people will not allow it. At the very top of that "punish the United States" list is Barack Obama.

Next, the Obama appointees at the Environmental Protection Agency (EPA) have been likened by some to be "eco-terrorists" in suits trying to cripple energy independence for our nation. If it's not "green" and already a proven failure, they don't want it.

As mentioned, nature does hate a vacuum, and if the United States of America is going to be foolish enough not to go after the oil in their own backyard, then the People's Republic of China—among others—is more than happy to step into the opening and literally suck oil out from the bottom of the sea, which originates within the sovereign territory of the United States.

While the current leadership of the United States willingly allows this to happen to appease spoiled eco-terrorists living off mommy and daddy's trust funds, the eventual leadership of our *new* Republic will *immediately* start to claim the oil off the coast of its new country, which will legally and rightfully belong to its citizens.

Beyond our desperately needed energy independence, next on the wish list is that all three states are *contiguous* and, because of their unique geographical position, they would lend themselves to not only better border security, but also to a better overall national defense should the need arise.

Next, the United States of America—meaning the hardworking taxpayers of our nation—have already made *massive investments* in the infrastructure of these three states. More than that, South Carolina, Georgia, and Florida each have a *significant military presence* in the form of Naval, Marine Corps, Air Force, Coast Guard, and Army bases, and these assets would be critical going forward as this new nation was formed.

In addition, these three states have climates that range from mild to tropical, which lends them to greater productivity year-round while creating a more stable environment for the inhabitants.

Next, collectively, South Carolina, Georgia, and Florida already have *millions of citizens* who share the fears and beliefs of our advisors. From that number will come the citizen foundation for this new Republic.

Ultimately, combined into one, the landmass of these three states would be very impressive and tops out at about 157,000 square miles. But, like most things in life, what is "impressive" is relative. Now, when compared to the 1,200 square miles of the state of Rhode Island, this new Republic would be truly huge. But, when compared to the likes of California (164,000 square miles), Texas (268,000 square miles), or Alaska (664,000 square miles), our new Republic starts—at least by territory—to look less impressive and maybe less foreboding by the mile.

But again, all of this is relative.

For instance, compared to the almost *3,800 million square miles* of the United States of America, our new nation and these other states look downright puny.

In sports and war, size sometimes does convey a real advantage. For instance, there is the old saying that goes, the bigger they are, the harder they fall.

That sounds nice, but when I played ice hockey, we had a more relevant and realistic saying: the bigger they are, the *harder* they hit.

That was true...sometimes.

To offset that reality and, since we're ticking off sayings, there's another that is entirely appropriate for comparison purposes: it's not the size of the dog in the fight, but rather the size of the fight in the dog.

Meaning...157,000 square miles will be plenty big enough if it is populated by those who—as those lyrics to the song "The Impossible Dream" say—are "willing to march into Hell for a Heavenly cause."

To our way of thinking, not only would this be a "Heavenly cause," but the land that would "theoretically" be inhabited is *blessed* as well.

Because we live in a "fast-food" country dumbing many down to a "fast-food" mentality, we tend to forget something critically important to our survival: supermarkets, electricity, running water, and "fast-food" establishments are relatively recent developments in the recorded history of humankind. For basically 99 percent of the six-thousand years of recorded history, we have been without these things. And guess what? They can be taken away again in a nano-second.

In many ways, precisely *because* of these "gifts" of modern life, we have grown fat, lazy, and ignorant.

We have *forgotten.*

We have forgotten that to feed, clothe, and house ourselves, *someone* has to grow the crops. *Someone* has to feed—and yes slaughter—the livestock. *Someone* has to grow, maintain, and cut the trees needed for our shelter.

For most in the United States of today, it's like magic. We drive to a supermarket, use a credit card to buy food already prepared, go back to a home already built, turn on the lights powered from…someplace, and then step into a shower cascading clean and abundant water from…someplace. Amazing.

And yet…we *forget*.

We forget that without the hard work—and often great sacrifice—of some fellow citizens, *none of that* would be possible.

We are blessed to have the farmers who feed us and with the land they use.

We are blessed with the technology we all take for granted.

We are blessed with the young men and women from our military who protect us.

We are blessed with dedicated police, firefighters, doctors, and nurses.

Again, all of this is a lifestyle that can be taken away from us instantly for a host of reasons, such as war, terrorism, natural disaster, or disease.

So…to build a country from the ground up…none of these things can or will be taken for granted. Life is very hard, and we have been so very spoiled over the last number of decades.

Those behind this project take *none* of our "gifts" for granted, nor do they think for a moment that these things can't be taken away from us. Again, the "power of negative thinking" put to positive use.

Knowing that, the states of South Carolina, Georgia, and Florida were chosen with great care and for incredibly practical reasons.

Because of the land and its very fertile nature, as well as the industries and impressive infrastructures, this new Republic would easily be self-sustainable in terms of producing the food, water, and commerce needed to nourish, employ, and protect the population.

SOUTH CAROLINA

The Palmetto State has a population of about 4.6 million and a coastline on the Atlantic Ocean of about 200 miles.

It also has about twenty-seven thousand farms, with each farm averaging about 200 acres with approximately 5.4 million acres of total farmland.

Forest covers about *two-thirds* of the state (over 12 million acres) with the timber industry being an essential part of the economy. South Carolina has total annual agriculture sales of about $3 billion. Cattle and calves are raised in every county in the state. Chicken production and sales are the state's top commodity.

Again, while none of us fortunate enough to be spoiled by supermarkets think about these things, within the state of South Carolina are about 250 million chickens, 8 million turkeys, 500,000 head of cattle, and 400,000 hogs.

The state also has a massive fruit and vegetable industry with some of its top crops being grain, oilseeds, beans, peas, rice, cucumbers, tomatoes, potatoes, and peaches.

It also has a very vibrant fishing industry.

As for *military installations*, the state is incredibly well represented: as a local website in the state proudly proclaims, it has a long and significant military tradition from the Revolutionary War to the present-day war on terror. The state has a significant number of military bases that provide a strong economic impact for the state and local communities. Many military retirees also choose to live in South Carolina for retirement. In fact, per capita, South Carolina has more military retirees living in the state than any other state in the United States.

What follows are brief descriptions as to how those military bases function now.

FORT JACKSON

Fort Jackson is located in the city of Columbia. Because of Fort Jackson, South Carolina has the largest Initial Training Center in the United States Army. It is at this location that 50 percent of all soldiers and 70 percent of all women entering the United States Army are trained.

SHAW AIR FORCE BASE

This important Air Force Base is located near Sumter and plays host to the Air Force's largest combat F-16 Wing. Additionally, it serves as home to Headquarters Ninth Air Force and United States Central Command Air Forces.

CHARLESTON AIR FORCE BASE

Located near Charleston, this base houses the 437th Airlift Wing, along with the 315th Airlift Wing (Reserves) flying massive C-17s in and out of the base on a regular basis.

MCENTIRE JOINT NATIONAL GUARD BASE

Located about 12 miles east of Columbia, this base is the proud home of the 169th Fighter Wing.

MARINE CORPS RECRUIT DEPOT PARRIS ISLAND

Located near Beaufort, South Carolina, and featured in numerous movies, Marine Corps Recruit Depot Parris Island is an 8,095-acre military installation tasked with the training of enlisted Marines.

MARINE CORPS AIR STATION BEAUFORT

Located about 70 miles southwest of Charleston, is the home of the Marine Corps' Atlantic Coast Fixed-Wing Fighter-Attack aircraft assets. The base sits on almost 7,000 acres.

NAVAL WEAPONS STATION CHARLESTON

Again, for the purposes of this book and this project, the base could not be more perfect. Located just outside of Charleston, it occupies over 17,000 acres, has over 16 miles of waterfront, four deep water piers, over 38 miles of railroad tracks and almost 300 miles of road.

COAST GUARD SECTOR CHARLESTON

This base serves as the regional operational command overseeing Coast Guard activities across South Carolina and Georgia. The "Sector" includes eleven field units and almost 1,700 active duty, reserve, civilian, and auxiliary personnel.

GEORGIA

Georgia has a population of about ten million with more coming to the state every day and a coastline on the Atlantic Ocean of about one hundred miles.

According to the University of Georgia and other sources, the agricultural industry plays a huge role in the state's economy. So much so, that it contributes *billions of dollars* annually to the state's economy. The main reason is that Georgia ranks first in the nation in the production of broilers (young chickens weighing less than two-and-a-half pounds), peanuts, and pecans.

Additionally, the Peach State ranks near the very top in the nation for acreage of cotton and rye, and the production of peaches, tomatoes, and tobacco. Georgia has more than 11 million acres of land dedicated to farming, with the average farm being almost 250 acres.

The poultry and egg industry alone account for almost $6 billion in cash receipts. More than 40 percent of the nation's peanuts and pecans are grown in Georgia. Beyond those crops, the state also contributes greatly with impressive amounts of hay, oats, soybeans, wheat, and greenhouse production.

There are almost twenty Fortune 500 companies headquartered in Georgia, as well as almost forty Fortune 1000 businesses. These are complemented by *thousands* of small businesses employing *millions* of people. Georgia's commercial transportation network includes 4,700 miles of railway, 118,777 miles of top-ranked public highways, *the world's busiest and most efficient airport* and air cargo leader, and *two deep-water sea ports* in Savannah and Brunswick, which presently ship to 153 countries.

Georgia is home to a significant number of US military bases and installations, all of which made it another logical state for the "S" Team to pick.

DOBBINS AIR RESERVE BASE
Located in Marietta, Georgia, the base is the home to the 94th Airlift Wing. The Wing is comprised of over 2,500 personnel with the base itself playing host to over twelve thousand people.

FORT BENNING
The world-famous Fort Benning has served as the home of the Infantry since 1918. It covers a massive 182,000 acres of land and sits in the "Tri-Community" areas of Columbus, Fort Benning, and Phenix City.

FORT GORDON
Located near Augusta, Georgia, the base is the home of the Signal Corps, the largest communications-electronics facility in the free world. It sits on over 56,000 acres.

FORT STEWART

Located on the East Coast of the state, Fort Stewart seems like the size of a small state with its approximately 280,000 acres of land. The fort is the home of the 3rd Infantry Division and is, in fact, the largest Army installation east of the Mississippi. The size of this base represents yet another reason why this state was included in our plans along with Florida and South Carolina.

MOODY AIR FORCE BASE

Located near Valdosta, Georgia, the base is the home to the 23d Wing and the 93d Air Ground Operations Wing.

NAVAL SUBMARINE BASE—KINGS BAY

One of the most important—and feared—bases in the world, Kings Bay is the East Coast home to the Ohio Class Submarines. In total, the Ohio Class Submarines carry over 50 percent of the active inventory of thermonuclear warheads for the United States. Each submarine carries twenty-four Trident II Missiles with each missile carrying up to sixteen warheads. While in Georgia, the base is located close to Jacksonville, Florida.

ROBINS AIR FORCE BASE

The base has the largest runway in the entire state of George and also serves as the state's largest industrial complex. It sits in the middle of the state and is about 100 miles south of Atlanta.

FLORIDA

Florida has a population of about twenty million people.

Because it has no state income tax and because of the socialist and crippling taxes such states such as New York, Illinois, Maryland, and California impose upon their job creators, hundreds of new millionaires and multimillionaires relocate to the Sunshine State every year.

In terms of agriculture, Florida is a national and international powerhouse. It produces about 80 percent of the oranges and grapefruits in the country, as well as most of the watermelons. Florida accounts for almost 50 percent of the world's orange juice supply. Its largest field crop is sugarcane and the second largest is peanuts. Overall, Florida is the second largest producer of vegetables in the nation.

There are more than forty-seven thousand farms in the state covering more than 10 million acres with the total agriculture revenue from all products—be they citrus, vegetable, sugarcane, or livestock—exceeding $10 billion annually.

More than 40 percent of all exports from the United States to Latin and South America pass through Florida. Florida averages about *90 million visitors per year* and it is the *number-one* tourist destination in the *entire world.*

What would a statistic like that mean for our new Republic? *Everything*, since tourism annually pumps about *$68 billion* into Florida's economy.

Overall, Florida has the fourth largest economy in the United States of America. Aside from the largest tourism industry in the world, it also has growing construction, international banking, biomedical and life sciences, aerospace, and defense. Not surprisingly, it is rated as one of the top states for business.

Also, of special importance considering the subject matter of this book, Florida has about 1,200 miles of coastline on both the Atlantic Ocean and the Gulf of Mexico. In addition to that incredible fact, it has more than 11,000 miles of rivers and waterways.

As a for instance, with Lake Okeechobee (more than 700 square miles), Florida has the second largest body of fresh water in the United States.

Aside from those many advantages to our project, the Sunshine State is also blessed with numerous military installations which would all play a role should the project move from the theoretical to the real.

Below is a snapshot of those bases.

MACDILL AIR FORCE BASE

Located almost in the shadow of Tampa, this base, which encompasses almost 6,000 acres, is the home of the 927th Air Refueling Wing, USCENTCOM, USSOCOM and thirty-five other Mission Partners.

The US Special Operations Command—or USSOCOM—again housed at MacDill—provides fully capable Special Operations Forces to defend the United States and its interests abroad. A major part of their portfolio is the synchronized planning of global operations against terrorist networks. Most recently, USSOCOM has operated in Iraq, Afghanistan, and anywhere where terrorist raise their heads and look toward our nation with bad intent.

EGLIN AIR FORCE BASE

With more than 724 square miles in the panhandle of Florida, this mammoth Air Force base is the home of the 96th Test Wing.

HURLBURT FIELD

Within shouting distance of Eglin Air Force base, Hurlburt Field is the home of the Air Force Special Operations Command as well as the 16th Special Operations Wing.

NAVAL AIR STATION—KEY WEST

Located in Boca Chica Key, it is a relatively small base with a big mission which is to support operational and readiness requirements for the Department of Defense, the Department of Homeland Security, the National Guard, various federal agencies, and allied forces.

NAVAL AIR STATION—PENSACOLA

This base is famous for many reasons, not the least of which being it is the home for the Blue Angels. Beyond that, every single Navy, Marine, and Coast Guard aviator has to train at this air station.

NAVAL AIR STATION—WHITING FIELD

Occupying almost 12,000 acres, it is also one of the Navy's top pilot training facilities in the country.

NAVAL STATION—MAYPORT

Located in the Jacksonville area, this critically important Navy base has a huge seaport as well as air facilities.

PATRICK AIR FORCE BASE

Located near Cocoa Beach, this base serves as home to the 45th Space Wing which manages all unmanned rocket launches out of the Cape Canaveral Air Force Station.

TYNDALL AIR FORCE BASE

Located near Panama City, this base hosts the 325th Fighter Wing, Air Combat Command. The wing consists of more than four thousand personnel who train and prepare F-22 Raptor pilots, intelligence officers, and other support specialties for worldwide assignment to combat Air Force unites. In total, the Wing provides support to more than twenty-three thousand Airmen, civilians, contractors, and their families.

* * *

Clearly, all three of these states have an incredible number of positives of which only a handful have been listed here. These positives would be the essential building blocks for the foundation of Traditional Values upon which a new Republic would stand.

As most of us understand, the building blocks are there and are ready to be assembled. The *only* ingredients missing at the moment are the men and women from those states, and every state across the country, willing to put aside all to start the construction of this new Union true to *their* beliefs.

Those patriots are out there and can be activated given the proper motivation.

We believe that motivation is coming.

CHAPTER 7

WHAT IF OTHER STATES WANT TO JOIN THIS NEW NATION?

opefully—and it's clearly a huge lift—if the "S" Team continues to do its outreach in the most effective manner possible and the building blocks of this recruitment drive continue to stack firmly one atop the other, then word should spread quickly within the population of the thirty million or so Americans who deeply believe in Traditional Values.

As that word goes forth about South Carolina, Georgia, and Florida becoming the territory of our new Republic, what then?

What if *other states* eventually—and *quite logically* as the All-Government United States of America would continue to crumble around them—decide they want to *join* the new Republic?

Two quick answers to that question:

First, as you can imagine, this is a question our team of advisors have explored from every possible angle. After analyzing all scenarios and each and every state that might lean toward making such a bold move, it was again the unanimous opinion of this group that unless the state wishing to join the new republic was *contiguous to the original three former states* of the United States of America, then it would not be allowed.

Meaning of course, the only new states that would—eventually—be considered in the near future would be North Carolina and Alabama.

It is not that other states would not be welcome. Quite the opposite, actually. But the advisors to this project strongly felt that if the states wishing to join the new Union were *not* contiguous, then they would present too many logistical problems from a territorial, border, and military perspective—in other words, massive headaches better left for later.

Secondly, for the time being at least, expanding the new Republic beyond the territory of the former states of South Carolina, Georgia, and Florida would not be practical. Our advisors strongly believe that the relative "small" size of our new Republic—again, about 157,000 square miles—makes it much more manageable and gives it a much greater chance of success.

As our advisors were meeting over a number of months to discuss this project, a question more than a few of them had was: What about Texas?

Indeed. What about Texas?

Again, for a number of very logical reasons, Texas seemed and seems like not only the perfect candidate to join a new Union, but in fact, to become a *new nation* all to itself.

To that very point, a 2013 article from the far-left *New York Times* accurately reported how despondent many resident of Texas were with the reelection of Barack Obama and how *passionate* those residents are about seceding from the Union. Said the article in part:

from **"White House Rejects Petitions to Secede, but Texans Fight On,"** by Manny Fernandez, for The *New York Times*, January 15, 2013

AUSTIN, Tex. — More than 100,000 people who signed an online petition calling on the Obama administration to allow Texas to secede from the United States and create an independent government received an official 476-word response from the White House last week.

The short answer was no . . . Obama administration officials were reacting to a flurry of secession petitions filed by residents of Texas and other states . . .

So again, what about Texas? It seems like the perfect candidate.

At first glance, that is.

From the Civil War era on, the proud people of Texas have long had an independent streak. More than that, they—be it Rick Perry or a number of homegrown conservative groups—have often speculated about, or mentioned, secession. Over the decades, that belief in secession has clearly and rightfully only grown for many Texans.

So, knowing this past and very recent history, some of the advisors to this project at first thought Texas would either be *the* candidate to become a new nation, or again, at the very least, one of the first states to join the new nation comprising the former states of South Carolina, Georgia, and Florida.

That was on first blush. On further reflection, the reason why this was not possible became *very* obvious to even the most ardent supporters of this idea.

In one word, the main and only real obstacle to this vision was *Mexico.*

For many Mexicans—and indeed many Texans—the Battle for the Alamo has never ended. *Never.* For a host of reasons, this is a very dangerous mindset.

The reality of today is that many politicians, military leaders, and elites of Mexico strongly believe that much of Texas and California is the territory of Mexico *stolen* from them by the United States of America.

The Mexican leaders who advance this belief are *not* a vocal minority. Within the government and the Mexican intelligentsia, they are a vocal *majority* and they adamantly believe that not only are large parts of Texas and California Mexican territory, but that it's only a matter of time before they forcibly take that land back from the United States of America.

This belief also permeates much of academia within Mexico and even filters its way down to the textbooks read by the children of Mexico. It's an indoctrination campaign that goes on daily within the country and is all but *unknown* or *ignored* by not only the vast majority of Americans, but also, dangerously, by most of our politicians and "leaders."

Beyond that almost declaration of war belief by much of the leadership of Mexico is the untenable border situation between Mexico and the United States.

As continually stressed, US politicians from both sides of the aisle long ago waved the white flag on *that* issue and literally *surrendered* our sovereign border to not only the government of Mexico, but to the drug cartels, the human traffickers, and even terrorists.

Why?

Again: pure self-interest. They made the conscious decision to sell out our national security in a naked attempt to pander for votes—votes not only from the Hispanic American community (ironically, the vast majority of these *legal* citizens appreciate and demand a closed and secure border with Mexico) but to win approval from the liberal elite in our country who advocate the borderless, "one-world" All-Government *theocracy* that has led to the downfall of the Traditional Values of the United States of America.

Consequently, the border between the United States of America and Mexico is a sieve, open to already happening *military incursions* from Mexico. Beyond the threats posed by the Mexican military, you have the drug cartels, which now openly rival the militaries of Mexico and the United States in terms of *lethal firepower.* After that, there is still the issue of the hundreds of thousands of Mexicans who cross the border illegally into the United States each and every year.

Knowing these daunting realities, it unfortunately becomes quite clear why Texas would not make a suitable independent nation, or even—for the moment—a candidate for joining our "theoretical" new Republic.

The complete southern land area of Texas borders Mexico. So again, aside from this untenable problem, is the ongoing issue of much of the leadership of Mexico openly salivating with the idea of *invading* Texas and taking back the territory "stolen from them" by the United States of America.

So, Texas "proper" could not join the new Union but...their highly valued citizens *could.*

Every single citizen of Texas—or any other state within the United States—would be welcome with open arms into our new nation infused with Traditional Values.

That is *the* point.

That is the crucial part of the, *for now*, academic exercise we are now exploring.

The members of the New Continental Congress will pursue these new citizens with a great and patriotic zeal.

Why?

To create the climate and conditions needed to set off the chain reaction that would culminate in the heretofore only imagined liberty in a heretofore only imagined new Republic.

CHAPTER 8

A NEW CONTINENTAL CONGRESS

The very first Continental Congress was held in Carpenter's Hall in Philadelphia from September 5 to October 26, 1774.

This Continental Congress was convened as the formal way the American Colonial governments would coordinate their *resistance* to the rule of the British Crown during the first two years of the American Revolution.

Almost 240 years later, many Americans believe it is well past time to convene a New Continental Congress—a New Continental Congress populated by men and women committed to liberty, faith, the rule of law, smaller government, and secure borders.

As has been outlined, only the states of South Carolina, Georgia, and Florida would (theoretically) serve as the landmass for our new Republic, the New Continental Congress would draw its members from all fifty states of the United States of America.

Any American who deeply believes in Traditional Values, and wants to explore the possibility of creating and living in a new country based upon those Traditional Values, would be strongly encouraged to participate in the entire process.

For planning purposes only, the members of the "S" Team have been reaching out to colleagues and friends in various states and asking them to compile a list of likely candidates from each state. These people in turn have reached out to their own lists and, as of this writing, are supremely confident they can recruit at least two hundred highly experienced and highly accomplished individuals from each state to help lead the process in the forty-seven states not designated as the land area for the new Republic as well as the three states that have been so designated.

A critically important part of this process for these volunteers would be to spread the word throughout their home state and then act as a clearinghouse for the residents in those states who would honestly and eagerly be willing to move to the new Republic when called upon.

The members of the "S" Team are under no delusions as to how incredibly tough all of this would be. They understand that under our 10 percent of the population of the United States of America model, it is *still* going to be slim pickings indeed.

If we rightfully assume that about thirty million Americans who deeply believe in Traditional Values no longer believe that the United States of America reflects their values and never will, it *still* does not mean—in any way, shape, or form—that these thirty million Americans would be willing to drop everything and move to a new Republic of their "dreams."

Not even close.

These Americans may have the strongest of convictions and they may have absolutely no doubts that all is lost in their present country. They may—and in fact, do—believe those things right down to their very core.

That said, even though they do, most, no matter what they say at the beginning, no matter how vigorously they nod their heads up and down that "secession is the only option left," most will still eventually decide against migrating into the new Republic.

Why?

Because they are *normal.*

Their fear of the unknown will eventually trump the certainty that they are living in a collapsing All-Government Nanny state. For "pragmatic" reasons—no matter how enthusiastic they were at first to sign up—most will decide the devil they know is better than the one they don't.

It may be a decision that sickens them inside precisely because of their values, but it *is* a decision most will make.

As the excitement of the dream of living in a true Traditional Values Republic wears off—and it will—most adults, and especially most parents, will start to second guess the whole process and wonder:

Is this really a pipe dream? Is it just a nice and distracting fantasy that will never come to fruition? What about my job? What about my home? What will I live on? How will I provide for myself and my children? What if it does become a reality and the government of the United States of America comes after us? Will there really be a military, or at least a Civilian Militia to protect us, our families, and our property? How would they do so?

The questions go on and each and every one is incredibly valid.

To be "willing to march into Hell for a Heavenly cause" often requires a complete leap of faith.

Most, no matter how hard they try, nor how much they think they believe, will not be able to muster up that leap of faith.

And guess what? That's okay. It's understandable and, as mentioned, it's quite normal. *Very* normal. Some would even argue that such a decision would demonstrate the very personification of *sanity.*

For those behind this project, we know that to be the case. We know most will opt out no matter what they say.

To use a sports analogy, if we look at the four major professional sports in our nation—basketball, football, baseball, and ice hockey—we know that tens of millions of young men have *no doubts*—zero—that they have what it takes to play one of those sports at the highest professional level.

They believe it . . . but they are wrong.

They simply don't have what it takes. Not even close. Not only are they lacking the purely athletic skills needed to ascend to that sports peak, but more importantly, they are lacking the mental toughness and mental certitude needed to outlast the competition and get to that level.

It has been proven that from all of the "exceptional" athletes playing these sports at the high school or college level, only 10 percent will be drafted. And from that 10 percent only 10 percent will make it to the National Hockey League, the National Football League, the National Basketball Association, and Major League Baseball.

Out of all the "truly exceptional" young athletes in the country playing these sports, only 1 percent will make it.

The other 99 percent certainly believed—at least for a fleeting moment—that they had what it took to realize their dream. But alas, they did not.

So . . . out of the *thirty million Americans* who "deeply believe in Traditional Values and are certain the United States of America has turned its back on them and their values forever," how many will *actually* make the required leap of faith needed to make a new Republic a reality?

Almost none.

We *know* that.

Again, it's that "power of negative thinking" thought process in action.

Going back to 1620 and the 102 brave souls who boarded the Mayflower for the "New World" free from oppression and persecution—what tiny percentage did *they* represent from all those who thought like them in England and Europe but were too afraid to step onto that ship?

What about the explorers who went before them and the settlers who came after? Each and every person *knew* they were taking the greatest risk of their lives. Every single person heard the stories about ship after ship full of men, women, and even children that sailed before them and *never* made it across the turbulent and highly mysterious Atlantic Ocean. Oftentimes multiple ships in a row didn't survived the crossing.

These people *knew* the odds were against them and yet they *still* boarded those ships. They still were willing to risk all they had ever known to either escape oppression and persecution or discover new lands.

Were these explorers, Pilgrims, and settlers "crazy"? Most assuredly many of their friends, neighbors, and even family members would have thought so and more than likely said so quite loudly.

And yet, in the face of such ridicule, in the face of such danger, in the face of certain death, they were the tiny percentage willing to pursue a dream with an act of courage almost no one back then was willing to follow through to its natural conclusion. These acts of courage eventually resulted in the discovery of the "New World," and the creation of the United States of America.

Such people and such acts of courage are understandably rare.

That's where the members of our New Continental Congress will play such a vital and pragmatic role. Each of the at least two hundred members of the New Continental Congress in all fifty states would be tasked with compiling an additional list of five hundred people.

The math then becomes quite simple and much more realistic: $200 \times 500 = 100,000 \times 50$ states $= 5,000,000$ people.

Meaning out of the thirty million Americans who deeply believe in Traditional Values and are positive the United States of America has turned its back on them and their values forever, only about 17 percent would actually take that leap of faith.

Or to frame that number another way, out of approximately 330 million Americans, only 1.5 percent of the entire population would risk everything to realize the dream of creating a new Republic built upon the foundation of "Traditional Values."

This means 98.5 percent would either strongly oppose the movement, be neutral, or strongly support it but decide at the last minute that they could not be the ones to make the longest leap of their lives.

So... is that number realistic? Is 1.5 percent of the nation ready to stand up and be counted when it comes to initiating and participating in a secessionist movement?

We believe so.

Can 1.5 percent of the entire nation really accomplish such an impossible dream?

Again, we believe so, as *we* will be salting the mine.

We believe so because from that number will come the best of the best—men and women who in a very real sense were pre-qualified by the members of our New Continental Congress. Men and women of uncommon valor. Men and women who have a track record of accomplishment. Men and women who have proven themselves time and again in the military, in business, in science, in medicine, and in all the fields needed to create a new Republic from the ground up. Men and women of unshakeable faith who have come to the conclusion, that for the good of all they love, no matter what anyone else decides, they *have to be* the ones to "march into Hell for a Heavenly cause."

CHAPTER 9

PEACE FROM STRENGTH: BUILDING A NEW NATION

Cleary, to create and build a new nation, we *will* need that experience, certitude, courage, a plan, and even a plan for when the "plan" does not go as planned.

Along with that, we will need treasure. Lots of "treasure."

Know that, the members of the "S" Team also identified and quietly reached out to a select group of people of *very* substantial means to take their temperature with regard to the project.

To their surprise, the reception was better than expected.

Much better.

Having created an estimate of the amount of money it would take to get the project up and running, the team specifically reached out to a number of entrepreneurs, small business owners, and large job creators in various states, including several billionaires. The more they heard about this "theoretical" option to the All-Government disease, which *is* killing the United States of America, the more they wanted to hear...well, more.

Contrary to what those who populated the Occupy Wall Street movement would have the naïve or ignorant believe, people of "means" more often than not *are* the financial backbone of this nation and do, one way or another, create *all* the jobs in our nation—most especially small business owners who, in turn, represent the backbone of business, for it is these small business owners who ultimate employ 80 percent of all Americans.

How ironic then that they and the other 1 percent of the "wealthy" are continually attacked by people who choose to *protest life rather than live life* and who *only tear down* and *never build*. Of course, it's also always conveniently amusing that when the Occupy Wall Street crowd does attack the "wealthy and uncaring 1 percent" from their own positions of comfort, wealth, or trust funds, they always leave such ultra-uber-wealthy liberals like George Soros, Steven Spielberg, Harvey Weinstein, Al Gore, Barack Obama, Barbra Streisand, Eric Schmidt, and Mark Zuckerberg off the list.

Leaving aside the dishonesty of the far-left—and make no mistake, to spout liberal mantra is to *knowingly* spout lies—there *are* hundreds of thousands of small business owners, entrepreneurs, millionaires, and even billionaires who strongly believe in Traditional Values and try to live their lives based upon those beliefs.

Just as both an experiment and a placeholder, the "S" Team identified more than four hundred business owners, entrepreneurs, millionaires, and even a few billionaires who stated that if the time ever came, they would not only enthusiastically move their business to the new Republic, but also help to *fund* as much of the logistical needs as possible.

This is a *big deal*, as nothing moves forward without the proper funding.

It is also important to keep in mind that this is just a relatively small sample done in a relatively short timeframe. There was little or no convincing needed to get these highly successful, highly educated, and deeply moral business leaders to agree to start writing checks when the time comes.

More than that, because these individuals have been so successful in the real world so far removed from "community organizing," they fully understood the tremendous obstacles before them and would be operating under no delusions.

To say that these impressive men and women are anxious to enter the fray would be an understatement. All are ready to "evangelize" and spread the word among other people of means because, as business leaders and job creators, they know the truth: it will take multiple millions of dollars more than the estimates to do this project correctly. The good news is they are confident they can bring the money to the table...and much more.

While the members of the "S" Team were somewhat surprised by the reaction of these friends and colleagues of "means," they should not have been. Once again, this was just "human nature" in action.

Successful people *do* develop, expand, and cultivate contact lists. This practice is part of their daily routine. Throughout the years, these experienced and accomplished business professionals not only easily recognized others in business who *think like them* with regard to Traditional Values, but made it a point to stay in *contact*.

No matter if there was ever a "secession movement," these very successful people still had the very human need to vent, to express their frustrations with, and deep fear of, the All-Government Nanny state.

Little did they or any of us realize that their Traditional Values contact lists already in existence could become the nucleus of something truly amazing.

Again, just with these small samples, we are talking about *multiple billions of dollars* hopefully pouring into the treasury of our new Republic.

Given that one of the main reasons Americans who believe in Traditional Values are convinced all is lost for the United States of America is our government's complete *abandonment* of *fiscal sanity*, the money and talent being pledged is a very good sign.

Lest we forget, our debt is something over *$17 trillion dollars*. The unbelievable wasteful and mysterious spending habits of our government cost upwards of $60 billion *per day*.

Of course, what's interesting to note about that mind-numbing figure is that, as of late, the government of the United States of America only has about $30 billion cash-on-hand.

This is not a *partisan* issue. It's an *American tragedy*.

Both political parties have contributed to the destruction of our economy.

Sometimes, for people to wrap their heads around a problem, you have to break it down into some basic components. Here are a few:

• Every single *day*, the national debt rises about *$4 billion*.
• Every single *day*, the United States Government borrows about *$5 billion*.
• The current national debt equals about *$50,000* for every man, woman, and child in the country or about *$140,000* per taxpayer.
• How much is a trillion dollars? It's *one thousand billion*. Or, a 1 with 12 zeros after it.
• Still not quite sinking in? Okay, how about this. If someone handed you $1 trillion and asked you to spend $1 *every second*—keeping in mind there are 86,400 seconds in a day and 2,678,400 in a month—it would take you more than *thirty-one thousand years* to spend the money.

- At $1 per second, it would *only* take you *527,000 years* to spend our current debt.

Clearly, an integral plank needed in the creation and building of a new nation is *financial stability.*

Those on the "S" Team with this specific portfolio felt there had to be consensus on two key issues. First, that our new Republic would operate on the Gold Standard, and second, that there would be a flat tax of some type.

Keep in mind that from the time of George Washington until 1971, the American dollar was linked to gold. A return to the Gold Standard is a return to monetary discipline.

One of the arguments against going back on the Gold Standard for the United States of America is that there's not enough gold in the world to cover our problems.

How much gold is there in the world?

While no one is really sure—as more is discovered each day—a rough estimate is about 175,000 metric tons. In dollar terms, that's somewhere in the neighborhood of $10 trillion. That's a good neighborhood, but not nearly good enough.

Again, when we stop to realize that our "leaders" have accumulated a debt of more than $17 trillion, it's easy to spot the problem in that math.

How bad is it in the United States of America with regard to *our* gold and *our* national debt created by *our* "leaders"?

Well, by some estimates, all the gold we have in Fort Knox equals about 8,200 metric tons. While the price of gold fluctuates daily, that gold equates to about $500 billion.

So, even if we took *all* the gold in the United States of America and liquidated it immediately to pay down our criminal national debt, then we would still be left with approximately $15.5 trillion in debt.

The United States of America is not only broken... but *broke.*

Is there any good news in those depressing numbers?

Yes, because the relatively small size of our new Republic works to our advantage. Based on the treasury of this project combined with the "theoretical" population, a Gold Standard could easily be maintained with the economy blossoming under such a fiscally sound program.

Another part of that "fiscally sound" program is the decision to immediately institute a flat tax in the new Republic.

Again, as we watch in horror as the Obama administration adopts the tactics of a police state by using the IRS to intimidate and silence not only its critics, but especially men and women of the Christian *faith,* it's easy to understand why an agency like that should never be replicated in the new Republic.

That understood, no one in the country or the world knows more about the flat tax nor is a better advocate for it than publisher Steve Forbes. He has proposed a 17 percent flat tax in the past with the details easy to find. Rather than recite those details here, however, it is much more important that we read his spot-on rationale for having a flat tax in the first place—a system more than thirty countries around the world have now made their own.

To this very point, Mr. Forbes authored a paper on the subject that should be required reading for every student and politician in the land. Below is part of that incredibly accurate article.

from **"The Moral Case for the Flat Tax,"** *AntiShyster News Magazine,* **1997**

Today's tax code is incomprehensible...It is the principle source of corruption in our nation's capital...Today, many of us view taxes as a form of legalized plunder; and we have little faith that the earnings we are forced to surrender to Uncle Sam will be used wisely or properly...

WHAT IS THE FLAT TAX?

The flat tax is a simple, fair, and uniform system with wide-spread support from Nobel Prize winning economists... *Time and again, evidence has shown government cannot preserve our families, reawaken our faith, restore our values, solve our social problems, or create prosperity. Only free individuals can.*

Powerful words that *crystalize* the issue of the moment...and our lives.

CHAPTER 10

THE COMING UNREST FOR THE NEW NATION: HOW BAD WILL IT GET?

To be sure, if our project ever went from the "theoretical" discussions now being held across the country, to the real, it would create a number of ripples—large and small—in the waters of our current government.

So, purely for the sake of "academic" discussion, we will assume that the project *is* real and *is* moving forward as envisioned by the "S" Team and those recruited to form that nucleus of the New Continental Congress.

Okay. Then what?

Well, as these three states eventually announce their plans to leave the Union and form a new nation based upon Traditional Values and the teachings of our Founding Fathers and then make known the very specific blueprint to accomplish this history-making—and earth-shaking—task, there *will be*—as stressed earlier and needs repeating—residents of these states who will strongly oppose such secession, just as there will be residents within these states who will strongly support this peaceful "revolution."

First, what can those who oppose the secession actually do?

Well, those residents in the states of South Carolina, Georgia, and Florida who oppose the secession would most certainly try to do all in their power—legal and otherwise—to delay or even stop the plan. *All options* that could be utilized by these protesting inhabitants *have been* anticipated and planned for by the group behind the nation-creating blueprint.

On the other side of that fence are all those *within* these three states who will *strongly support* this peaceful revolution knowing they will quickly be joined and fortified by millions more from around the nation who covet freedom and those Traditional Values and would be desperate to join these new citizens in their new country free from the destructive hands of the All-Government Nanny state.

In many ways, it would become the most important geo-political chess game of our lives.

As mentioned, as the movement goes forward, it would be critical that those behind this particular project anticipate, understand, and have responses in place to deal with each and every question and the expected opposition.

Regarding that expected opposition, what would be the first course of action from those committed to shutting down this secessionist movement?

Without a doubt, it will be the courts: local, state, federal, and finally, the Supreme Court.

Two points here: First, as very accurately addressed by Dr. Brion McClanahan earlier in "Is Secession Legal?" (TheAmericanConservative.com, December 2012): ". . .once the States have seceded from the Union, the Constitution is no longer in force in regard to the seceded political body. This same rule applies to the Article I, Section 10 argument against secession. If the Constitution is no longer in force—the States have separated and resumed their independent status—then the Supreme Court would not have jurisdiction and therefore could not determine the 'legality' of the move.

The Union, then, through a declaration of war could attempt to force the seceded States to remain, but even if victorious that would not solve a philosophical issue. War and violence do not and cannot crush the natural right of self-determination."

That said, the second point is there is *no doubt* that the "leaders" of the United States will go whining to their courts begging them to "please stop these Traditional Values people...whoever they are and wherever they come from...from leaving us to go live in freedom from our Tyranny. Please."

As we anticipate and prepare for this predictable attack, we would all be well served to once again think back to 2012 presidential election. As in, the election a *few million* conservatives and men and women of faith decided to sit out for various reasons. As we do focus on that incredibly important fact, those who believe in Traditional Values must never forget one thing: sitting out an election will *always* have consequences.

While one should never vote for a person whose values run counter to your own, it should still be understood that "non-votes" play as much or even a greater role in the outcome of an election.

Back in 2012, because millions of conservative and Traditional Values voters found the Republican nominee lacking in so many areas, they did choose to stay home rather than vote for a candidate they believed to be less than committed to their beliefs and seemingly a tool of the entrenched GOP establishment.

That's fine and that's their prerogative and right, but whether they want to admit it, that decision *had* and *has* consequences.

In golf, they say every shot makes someone happy. This means, of course, if the player hits a good shot, he is happy. If he hits a bad shot, his opponent is happy.

The same philosophy applies to politics and most especially presidential elections.

If conservatives choose not to vote because the "conservative" candidate does not reflect their values, then the "liberal" candidate and his or her supporters are of course going to be very happy because of this rightfully debatable choice.

Should that liberal candidate go on to win by a relatively close margin—as was the case in the 2012 presidential election—then the liberal candidate will obviously reap the rewards of his success.

Clichés become clichés because, more often than not, they reflect all or a large part of the truth. Understanding that, we must then focus on the "cliché" of the moment that speaks to this dilemma—the one that asks about the lesser of two evils.

Knowing that all elections do have consequences and that oftentimes of late almost every vote *does* seem to count, when do conservative and faith-based Americans put principle aside—or at least aspects of it—to then vote for the lesser of two evils?

A better question is: *Should* people of faith who have built their lives upon that foundation of Traditional Values *ever* put principle aside to vote for the lesser of two evils?

At one time or another, we all have or will be confronted with that question and each person must decide for themselves.

As for me, my answer would be an unequivocal no. I don't believe principles can *ever* be compromised, watered-down, or ignored.

Yet, the compromising of principles is the norm in Washington. It has become the *coin of the realm*. It's what our politicians do for recreation in our nation's capital. That dangerous weakness is one of the few things almost all our elected officials have in common. Day by day, week by week, and month by month, politicians from both sides of the aisle compromise themselves and *our* principles for *their* greater good. And, year by year, most elected officials sell out themselves—and us in the process—to either pad their bank accounts, get reelected, please the "leadership" of their party, or cater to lobbyists dangling campaign donations or future well-paying jobs in their faces.

In my opinion, and the opinion of everyone advising on this book, the compromising of principles is *exactly* what got us in this mess in the first place. The United States of America as we once knew it and loved it has all but ceased to exist because *most* of our elected officials are in it for themselves, their parties, their unions, or the lobbyists pulling their strings.

Which politicians are truly in it for the people? Virtually none.

If Washington *were* populated by men and women of principle, character, and integrity, there would be no need for this book and no need for any type of secessionist movement.

Sadly, that is not the case—far from it, actually.

Washington and most of our state and local governments are populated by hedonistic politicians who have long since stopped caring about right and wrong, the inspiring words of our Founding Fathers, and most importantly, the will and the welfare of the American people.

So, no. For me, I don't believe that principles should *ever* be compromised.

That said, for those of us who choose never to compromise our principles—a decision that often sees us vilified by the entrenched establishment of the Republican Party—what are *we* to do?

If we are *not* going to compromise then it *is* incumbent upon us too stand up, be accountable, and *do* something.

Here's a wild thought: maybe start a *new* country based *entirely* on our principles.

Until that day comes, however, it's wise to remember that good people of faith and values can and do disagree on this issue. In 2012, for instance, tens of millions of Americans held their nose and voted for the Republican nominee *only* because they thought he was the lesser of two evils.

Good for them. But, as they say, the lesser of two evils is *still* evil, and millions of others Americans of principle felt that way.

Obviously, for these other Americans, voting for the lesser of two evils was and never will be an option. To do so would be to vote against all they hold dear.

But, as stressed, those millions of "non-votes" also have and had consequences.

Those of us willing not to vote to honor our faith and conscience must also be willing to admit and accept that the "non-votes" played a significant role in the reelection of the far-left president who now occupies the Oval Office.

We must acknowledge that to the victor go the spoils—many, many spoils, some much more critical than others. One of those critical spoils for the victor is the courts.

Or more precisely, the opportunity to "pack the courts."

Most Americans and too many conservatives tend to think of the "courts" as only the Supreme Court. Not only is that view shortsighted and wrong, but it is also injurious to the welfare of our nation.

Once again, we need to remind ourselves that the far-left and many Democrats look at politics, policy, and the ability to make law as a full-contact sport. And a blood sport at that. They are in it to win it and to win it at *any* cost.

These far-left zealots must never be underestimated. Or to be more precise, they *never should have been* underestimated. For the last few decades, conservatives and men and women of faith—again for credible and good reasons—have done nothing *but* underestimate the viciousness of the far-left.

That said, they did so at their and *our* risk.

Hence, the deplorable and dangerous state of our nation and the need for this book—a book that will hopefully add to the dialog and debate already taking place, a dialog that is quickly leading to a unique window in time to at least *explore* the possibility of secession. How much that window opens and how long it will remain open rests in the hands of our current government, all of the American people, and a handful of patriotic Americans assessing the current situation and feverishly working behind the scenes to determine if and when they should act.

And *if* they act... *how?*

So, going back to the spoils of the courts, while most Americans and conservatives only think of the Supreme Court when they hear the phrase *packing the court*, to the far-left, it means so much more.

As in, pack the nine circuit courts, as well.

Why?

Because the far-left understands that the party, or more accurately, the "ideology" that controls these courts, holds much of the fate of the nation in their hands.

These federal courts, just like the Supreme Court, are lifetime appointments and carry immense and often irrevocable power. *Irrevocable.*

Voting is a privilege and often considered a "civic responsibility" by many conservatives and Americans of faith—as it should be, at least in a nation that used to play by the rules.

But, to stress one more time, to the victor do go the spoils. An invaluable and lasting segment of those "spoils" is the ability—in this case—to install liberal, All-Government, politically correct–enforcing, anti–Traditional Values—*judges* in positions of great power and lasting influence—a negative influence that affects the lives of generations to come.

But, as we also talked about earlier, many from the far-left—be they politicians, union leaders, professors, entertainment executives, journalists, historians, or even *federal judges*—are *very* predictable. You *can* expect them to do the worst.

So, from the White House down to the circuit courts, they will do all in their power to not only "legally" stop the secessionist movement, but also, more than likely, they will seek to vilify or even *arrest* the leadership and put them on trial.

If the movement is successful in exposing and thwarting the kangaroo court of the far-left, what then? What action or series of actions will the far-left next attempt to take to stop the *legal, peaceful, and constitutional* secessionist movement?

* * *

Beyond the legal actions and shenanigans the government of the United States of America might try to unjustifiably use to enforce authority it *no longer has*, what else *might* they try as our new Republic becomes a reality?

Would they *dare* go the military route? It is a question that *must* be asked and anticipated.

Would the president, his—or her—White House, administration, and the Congress—with the biased backing of the mainstream media—"speak" for the remainder of the United States of America and order a military strike against the now new Traditional

Values—observing nation made of the former states of South Carolina, Georgia, and Florida? Would they *really* go that far?

Would *any* future president and *any* future Congress attempt to start the next "Civil War" in our nation by ordering federal troops to literally fire on their brothers, sisters, mothers, fathers, and other relatives?

If it came to that, how would these federal troops react to such an order? Would they obey a commander in chief who is asking them to attack people who, in their minds, are not only innocent, but simply trying to live their own lives in a peaceful and legal manner? People who, a few short weeks or months ago, were fellow citizens of the United States and were now—at the very least—still friends and relatives?

Should the commander in chief somehow find such troops willing to declare war on this new nation of true liberty and fire on family and friends, what then?

Would our new nation, built on the foundation of Traditional Values, be able to defend itself from such an unwarranted and illegal attack? How could it possibly stand up against the military might of the still most powerful nation on the planet Earth?

CHAPTER 11

THE DEFENSE OF A TRADITIONAL VALUES NATION—HOW MUCH IS ENOUGH?

A s this secession from the United States of America would be done in a completely legal and transparent way, it is believed by the group behind the blueprint that other than legal challenges—of which there would be many and those would be immediate—the government of the United States of America would be *powerless* to stop the transformation.

That said, there's really never anything wrong with asking, what if?

As highlighted already, I am a *big believer* in the "power of negative thinking." With this project, hopefully the "worst case" never materializes but, if it does, at least you have envisioned it, understood the ramifications of it, and potentially war-gamed a few Houdini-like escapes out of the trouble.

So, as long as we are talking about What-ifs that will *never* happen, then there's no harm in asking, what if the government of the United States of America decides—much like Abraham

Lincoln—that it needs to go beyond legal persuasion to attempt to get our new nation back into the fold?

Well for starters, that's where a good portion of the Second Amendment would kick in. You know, the Amendment that still thankfully exists as *originally written* and says, "A well-regulated Militia, being necessary to the security of a free state, the right of the people to keep and bear Arms, shall not be infringed."

The truth is, our Founding Fathers considered a well-armed militia a necessity and that it was the *civic duty* of each and every male to possess a gun and *participate* in the militia.

In our new Republic, it would be the civic duty of any and all adults who so chose to possess a gun and participate in *our* new militia.

As former governor and presidential candidate Mike Huckabee said at 2014's Conservation Political Action Conference, "I know that the Second Amendment is the only last resort we have in this country to protect all the other freedoms that we enjoy."

Tens of millions Americans strongly agree with Governor Huckabee and, hopefully, a solid percentage of them would be moving into our—as of now—fictional new Republic.

With this exact reality now in mind, many of these same Americans know well the history and the legend of the Sons of Liberty.

If you or I were to end up as *active members* of the secession movement, what would the current government of the United States of America label us? What would the far-left and their propagandists in the mainstream media call us?

Traitors?

Interesting. If those who would label us such had been around during the time of the American Revolution, what would they have labeled men like John Adams, John Hancock, Patrick Henry, and Paul Revere?

All of those men—and thousands more who helped to free us from the British Crown—were members of the Sons of Liberty, a group loosely started in 1765 in and around Boston, but by the end of that year, the Sons of Liberty were in *every* Colony.

These four American heroes and patriots were a part of this group. They were members of a secret organization set up only to *defend the rights of their fellow Colonists* being oppressed by a massive government over-taxing, over-regulating, under-representing, and threatening them all.

Would Barack Obama have called them *extremists*? A word he likes to throw around quite a bit when he is trying to describe conservatives or Christians.

Would the far-left blogs and "news" sites have called these heroic patriots *traitors*?

Everyone reading this book—even those who inexplicably still support Mr. Obama—know the honest answer to that question.

They would call us traitors and much, much worse.

Should all the legal options of the government of the United States of America fail—and they *would*, as we have the Constitution of the United States of America still on our side and the constitutional experts advising the project to back up that defense—then common sense dictates we at least try to anticipate what steps the US government would take to eliminate what many on the far-left—or again that corrosive entrenched establishment—would most certainly perceive to be a direct threat to the freedom-eradicating Nanny state they have taken years to install across virtually every segment of society.

So, after failing in the courts—even some of the handpicked justices of the far-left would be unable to rule against the clearly spelled-out law of the Constitution—there is every reason to expect the now adversarial United States of America to at the very least *explore* military options to try and bring our new nation to "its senses" and back within its borders.

Should that be the message sent in the strongest possible vocal terms from the former "Mother Ship," what then the response from our new nation?

Even the very thought of standing up to the most powerful military the planet has ever known elicits the very logical question: Are we crazy?

How would this tiny new nation of three former states defend itself against the biggest and baddest country in the world?

It couldn't... *right?*

Years ago, when I was a child, I had a poster in my bedroom that read: "Yea, thou I walk through the valley of the shadow of death, I will fear no evil for I am the meanest son-of-a-bitch in the valley."

Now, while our new nation can never match the almost incalculable military power of the United States of America, it *can* trump the US government in the meanness and *crazy* department. For its survival, this new nation would almost assuredly have to *dial-up* the calculated insanity... if needed.

If we buy into the "meanness" and "crazy" defense, then what next? How do we make those intangibles work for us?

First, by making it clear beyond the shadow of *any* doubt that this new nation created on the territory of these three former states of the United States has brought and further developed the means to defend itself against *any* attack.

As Eddie Murphy's character demonstrated in the first *48 Hours* movie, you can make a point and even great progress with "bullshit and a badge." You can get even further if you can and *will* back up the "bullshit" with the real deal.

As war-gamed by the advisors behind this project, in the area of national defense, nothing will be left to chance and "bullshit" will just be one small arrow in a relatively powerful quiver of military options.

That "quiver" of national defense will have many components giving the leadership of *our* new nation *viable* options—options that would quickly be made very clear to the US government.

What options? There will be many, but the first that will be mentioned to the leadership of the United States would be that our new nation has acquired some of the top military, intelligence, and counter-terrorism experts in the world. Beyond that, it is also staffed with a cadre of some of the most cutting-edge scientists operating on the planet—*nuclear* and otherwise.

Within the framework of these discussions with the leadership of the United States of America, it will become quite evident that the leadership of our new nation also has more than a few tricks up its sleeve. As to what these tricks might be—read *weapons systems* and other *tactical* options—much of that will be much better left to the hopefully fertile imagination of the leadership of the United States of America.

Again, all of this has been fleshed out in a totally "theoretical" atmosphere.

Once that "theoretical" reality was made clear to the government of the United States—and once it was truly convinced—and it *would be*—that the new nation was serious and *would* do all in its power to protect itself and its peace-seeking citizens—then the US government would have to do a cost analysis to determine how much pain and destruction it would be willing to absorb should it launch what, by any and all rational thought and law, would be an *illegal* and *totally unprovoked attack* against our Traditional Values–espousing nation.

More than that, the government of the United States of America would have to ask itself if it was *truly prepared* to potentially *slaughter* tens of thousands of innocent men, women, and children who—though they now reside in this new Republic—are *still* the sons, daughters, grandchildren, grandparents, cousins, friends, colleagues, and former neighbors of the remaining population in the United States.

Talk about an international war crime.

CHAPTER 12

REAGAN: A NEW REPUBLIC IS NAMED

What's in a name? In this case... *everything*.

It was also the unanimous consensus of our team that until the people—in conjunction with the New Continental Congress—can vote, the interim—and maybe permanent—name for the new nation created upon the foundation of Traditional Values would be named after, and honor, President Ronald Reagan.

In many ways, the name of this new nation was one of the *most* perplexing assignments faced by the men and women behind this—*until now*—highly confidential project.

With regard to the new nation—and as has been said in the past—an awful lot is going to swing on this hinge—as in, the *entire* weight of liberty for a few million people desperate for freedom.

This means, of course, that for all those inside and outside of our new nation, its actual name is going to have great significance and the deepest of meanings, both for very good reasons and for reasons—totally unfounded—of ongoing concern.

The advisors felt the name itself had to speak volumes the second anyone heard it or read it. The name had to convey the deep-seated *beliefs and intentions* of the inhabitants of our new Republic.

Upon hearing or reading the name, it had to send an instant message far and wide. For our team of advisors, this message—*our message*—had to be as unambiguous and crystal clear as possible. It *had* to be a message of *hope.*

For our advisors, that message of hope is everything. It is why they agreed to participate in this project in the first place. They also felt they had to be part of something larger than themselves—something that would speak to their own concerns and fears, and then at least through their very best intentions and efforts, offer some timely and tangible solutions that could be enacted in the future—something that would then be debated, dissected, vilified, and cheered by those in and out of the United States of America paying attention to our rapid and irreversible decline.

For all of those reasons and many more, our advisors felt the naming of this new nation was a *solemn responsibility* that would have ramifications for decades to come.

Recognizing what that meant, that—as with every subject associated with this *history-making* cause—there was plenty of active and animated debate regarding the—for now—*theoretical* creation and naming of this new nation.

It was a debate that suddenly subsided almost as quickly as it started when the solution dawned on almost all at once.

As it will be the *people's* country, it will be a name eventually chosen *by* the people.

Men and women infused with Traditional Values who, as we keep saying—and against all odds—broke from the pack and sure-footedly stepped into that arena so eloquently framed over a century ago, by Teddy Roosevelt.

As it is a speech and a message that should never be forgotten, it bears repeating:

During his remarks titled "Citizenship in a Republic"—now much better known as the "Man in the Arena" speech—delivered at the Sorbonne in Paris on April 23, 1910, Teddy Roosevelt crystallized the thoughts of all those willing to fight for what is right no matter the cost. Said the then-president:

> It is not the critic who counts; not the man who points out how the strong man stumbles, or where the doer of deeds could have done them better. The credit belongs to the man who is actually in the arena, whose face is marred by dust and sweat and blood, who strives valiantly; who errs, who comes up short again and again—because there is no effort without error and shortcoming—but who does actually strive to do the deeds; who knows great enthusiasms, the great devotions; who spends himself in a worthy cause; who at the best knows in the end the triumph of high achievement, and who at the worst—if he fails—at least fails while daring greatly, so that his place shall never be with those cold and timid souls who neither know victory or defeat.

Amen.

For the men and women to whom that speech resonates, they decided they could no longer timidly sit on the sidelines wringing their hands with despair while they watched helplessly as the country they grew up in and loved so deeply was desecrated and destroyed by the socialist underpinnings of the All-Government Nanny state.

The advisors behind this project felt that, at the very least, if things move forward and become real, that these incredibly courageous men and women had earned the right to name *their* new nation.

For without these millions of individuals who decided to throw caution to the wind and band together for the most imposing and high-minded of causes, there would be nothing. *Nothing.*

For these citizens, their children, our advisors, and all who cherish true liberty free of the suffocating restrictions of the All-Government, it is the chance to step into that arena or lose all we hold dear.

Under the *growing* totalitarian dictates of the All-Government, we are given just enough to exist while being pushed along like lemmings toward the cliff.

Understanding the very finality of that threat, the men and women who would voluntarily step into this most valorous of arenas are the new centurions of liberty. They are the new guard.

They—and *you*—are the true patriots of today. Back in 1773, the Massachusetts Sons of Liberty chose to make their voices heard by dumping 342 crates of tea into the Boston Harbor as a way to protest the growing British imperialism.

Today, the fight is *infinitely* more important.

Back in 1773, it was a battle against King George and a foreign nation.

Now, tragically and quite surreally, it is a fight against *our very government.* The All-Government—a government that, over a number of decades, has been allowed to grow beyond all reason, to become the number-one threat to liberty.

Hence, this project, this at least theoretical fight against the All-Government with the culmination in the creation of a new nation, a new nation of liberty, of laws, of security, of faith, and of the smallest government possible.

For the advisors behind this project, it became clear that the people, and *only* the people of our new nation, could and should choose its permanent name. But these advisors also recognized that there would be an interim period between the establishment of our new nation and the time when all things were in place to hold a referendum on the name of the new Republic.

So, what to do during that time period? What temporary name could be given to this new nation until the people chose the permanent one?

For our advisors, there was only the one choice:

REAGAN

The place-holder name—unless the people choose to make it permanent—of this new land of true liberty would be named after President Ronald Reagan, a man who literally personified everything represented by our new nation and the honorable men and women who dreamed of it, who created the blueprint, who chose to step into the arena to fight for it, and who will live in it. The Republic's people would be desperate to live peacefully in a nation true to their values and the values of the forty-second President of the United States of America.

So, The Republic of Reagan it is: a shining city atop the hill that might one day serve as the *last remaining* beacon of hope in the world for all those desperate to be free from tyranny.

* * *

As for me personally, the name Reagan has added significance, as the *highest honor of my professional life* was serving as a writer for President Ronald Reagan in the White House during his last years in office.

During that remarkable time, I was afforded the unique privilege of having an incredibly real and lasting conversation with

President Reagan in the Oval Office, a conversation about a painful subject that had affected us both negatively...and positively.

Several weeks into my new position, I was sitting in my tiny cubicle in the Old Executive Office Building—part of the White House complex which houses 90 percent of the White House staff—when the phone rang. I picked it up and identified myself. A second later, the voice on the other end of the line said, "Mr. MacKinnon. This is White House Signal calling. The president of the United States would like to speak with you."

One second later, President Ronald Reagan was on the other end of the phone line. As he spoke, I tightened my grip on the handset as I felt it slipping from the waterfall I was creating in the palm of my left hand.

While most of the conversation was a blur, I do remember he thanked me for defending him in a recent column and asked if there was anything he could do for me.

While the public may not know or believe it, just because you work at the White House or even on the president's staff, does not mean you ever get to meet him, at least not back then. Nowadays, all presidents host "holiday" parties—we live in a nation that is 80 percent Christian and even the White House— "The People's House"—refuses to say "Christmas" purely for cowardly reasons of political correctness—where the staff can get their photo taken in a long line that affords the staffer five seconds with the president. Back in the day, when I worked for President Reagan at the White House, employees like me didn't always get that perk.

So, knowing this might be my one and only chance to meet the president, I pulled together my courage, closed my eyes, and stammered out, "Mr. President, I would be greatly honored to have a photo taken with you in the Oval Office one of these days."

Ronald Reagan, the president of the United States, let out a quick chuckle at my nervous request and answered, "Of course. I'll have Kathy make the arrangements."

Several days later, my personal rendezvous with history arrived. I was standing outside the door of the Oval Office, sweating like Albert Brooks in the movie *Broadcast News*.

Suddenly, the door to the Oval Office swung open and a presidential protection division agent from the United States Secret Service waved me in. As I walked in, the president stood up from behind his desk and walked toward me. We met in the middle of the Oval Office and the president greeted me with a warm smile and an extended right hand.

At least for me, everything was surreal and moving in slow motion. My knees felt more than a bit wobbly as the president's hand wrapped around mine. I could not believe that I was in the West Wing of the White House and had just entered the Oval Office by invitation of the president himself.

I tried to calm myself by remembering that Ronald Reagan— like me—was a very spiritual man who had a deep belief in Jesus Christ and His traditional teachings.

Remembering that produced a small smile on my face as my mind fleetingly focused on two tests I would always use when faced with a tough dilemma. If the dilemma was spiritual, I would always ask myself "What Would Jesus Do?" If the dilemma was political, I would always ask myself "What Would Ronald Reagan Do?"

As long as I answered both questions honestly, I always did fine.

Ronald Reagan was not only a man of great faith, but at one time, had been one of the "great unwashed masses." He never forgot where he came from and would never think not to figuratively and literally reach out a hand to those who most mattered to God.

President Reagan was often kidded by the elites for wearing brown suits from time to time. He was also credited by others as being the "only man on Earth who looked great in a brown suit." On this particular morning, the president looked more than dapper in his dark brown suit, crisp white french-cuff shirt, and soft red tie. As red was his wife Nancy's favorite color, he enjoyed wearing red ties whenever possible.

The president's handshake was very firm while his hand was soft and dry. Unfortunately for him, I instantly changed that. Just before walking into the Oval Office, I had uselessly wiped my palm one last time on my pant leg. By the time my hand rested in the president's, it had once again produced enough moisture to drown a small rat.

President Reagan paid no attention to my problem and instead looked me straight in the eye, and with a twinkle in his, actually gave me his famous, "*Well*...it's nice to finally meet you, Doug."

Many times, when staff or outsiders enter the Oval Office for the first time, they comment later that it—or the president—seemed "smaller than expected." While at six-foot-two, I had an inch or two on the president, he and the Oval Office seemed immense. Ronald Reagan's stature, reputation, power, and warmness seemed to fill the room like nothing I had ever encountered before.

I looked down at the president's hand wrapped around mine and then back up at him and sheepishly said, "It's an honor to meet you, Mr. President. I hope I wasn't out of line asking for a photo."

The president kept his smile intact as he slowly shook his head, placed his hand on my back, and gently turned me to face a photographer.

After a flurry of photos, the president turned back to look at me and his face got a bit more serious.

"Doug. I want to thank you for writing that column. Maybe some people think because it's the end of my second term, I don't matter anymore. I hope not. But regardless, it's nice to know that there are some young people like you out there who still think I do a few things right."

"More than some, Mr. President. There are millions of us out there who won't forget what you've done for this country and world. You're the role model for how all politicians should behave."

He tilted his head to the side, tightened his lips, and said a simple, "Well...thank you."

Just then, a door that led from the Oval Office to his assistant's office opened and I knew my time with the president was coming to a rapid close. I had rolled the dice to get here and was, at that very second, fighting a furious battle within my mind as to whether I should make the observation that was begging to get out.

As I did during the phone call, I decided to throw caution to the wind and just go for it. For all I knew, this would be the first and last time I got a chance to have a real conversation with the president of the United States and, if my childhood of abject poverty and being homeless from time to time had taught me anything, it was that it is almost always better to ask for forgiveness than permission.

Growing up with less than nothing and living in cars makes you much more open to risk. What's the worst they could do to me? Certainly nothing worse than what I had experienced up until that moment.

Since working for President Reagan, I had come to learn that his father was basically the town drunk in Reagan's hometown of Dixon, Illinois. Ronald Reagan, his mother, and his brother were subjected to the usual taunts, insults, heartbreak, and desperation that come from living with a serious alcoholic. His dad was almost like Otis from the old *Andy Griffith Show*, and it tore him apart almost every day of his young life.

Knowing all of that background, I looked at the president, took a deep breath, and said, "Mr. President. I know I have to leave in a minute, but I wanted to take a moment to tell you that I understand how much you've overcome and what you've accomplished. My father has the same problem now that your dad did when you were a child and I just felt it was important to tell you that."

There. I said it. I half expected the president to be offended with the comparison. Instead, it was if, for the first time during our brief visit, he took stock of who was standing before him. The smile left his face, his eyes seemed to narrow just a notch, and he stepped closer to me.

"How so?" he asked in almost a whisper.

I gave him a thirty-second history of my family life and the problems my dad and mom had with alcohol, and by the time I was done, I was shocked and heartened to see tears in the eyes of the president of the United States. I could not believe it. Not only had I just said something that had real meaning to this president, but I had also said something that clearly reawakened in him some memories from his own troubled childhood.

Because this meeting was *so* personal and meaningful to me, the president's surprise emotion took things to a new and much higher level. As I felt tears fill my eyes, I was not in the least bit ashamed or embarrassed. All the opposite, in fact. I was in the presence of a man who not only got it...but who had *lived* it.

When you are a child of an alcoholic—or alcoholics, in my case—you live your childhood behind a wall of invention, deception, and fear. You will go to the greatest lengths to ensure that your ugly little secret is not discovered by friends, classmates, or neighbors. As discussed, you learn to act at a very young age to stave off the dreaded humiliation that you know comes with exposure. As I looked at Ronald Reagan, I had no doubt he was thinking of exactly the humiliation that is a constant companion of the children of alcoholics.

As the president's face visibly softened and he and I both instantly dropped those protective shields, I wondered to myself what role his father's drinking played in his accomplished acting ability. Because of his childhood, I had no doubt that he—as the actor Michael Caine related in his own memoir—had begun to hone those skills at a very young age. It went with the territory.

With the kindest of empathy and caring, the president stepped even closer—as if to keep my secret safe and ensure he was out of earshot of the Secret Service Agent, the photographer, and his assistant—and whispered yet again, "Children can be so cruel at times."

Amazed by, and emotional from, the true kindness of the man before me, I slowly nodded my head and held out my hand to say thank you and goodbye.

Instead of taking my hand, Ronald Reagan stepped closer and gave me a protective hug because of the bond we now shared.

So, yes...his name...his reputation...and his beliefs mean everything to me.

Like tens of millions of Americans, I have no doubt that he was *our greatest president and greatest leader.*

As such, I—along with the advisors working on this project behind the scenes—gave the utmost thought and respect to the assignment of deciding the interim name of this new Republic. In our minds, it could be nothing else.

CHAPTER 13

NEXT STEPS

A TRADITIONAL VALUES–ESPOUSING NATION MAKES ITS MARK AND THE WORLD TAKES NOTICE

If...and when...the Republic of Reagan is created, its strict and needed adherence to our Traditional Values, coupled with peace, prosperity, coexistence, and friendship, *will* make it that true beacon of *hope* to human beings the world over crushed under the heavy boot of tyranny.

Okay, for the sake of *our sanity* and in the name of *that hope*, let's agree that a new Traditional Values Republic *will be* established and will be known throughout the world as Reagan.

Now what?

In a perfect world or in a happy ending Hollywood script, it would be everlasting peace and prosperity forever.

Clearly, neither a perfect world nor country exist and ultraliberal Hollywood got out of the "happy endings" business years ago in favor of bashing Christians, conservatives, our intelligence operatives, and the US military...all for a profit, of course.

So, back to reality—but a reality we are working to reshape. That reality tells us that precisely because the world we inhabit is so morally and ethically challenged, our new Republic of Reagan will shine and succeed like no other nation on Earth.

Why?

Because the *truth* will finally be on full display for all to see, a truth that will either inspire or petrify, depending on which side of the ideology and values people hold.

Much of that truth will outright shred the propaganda falsehoods of the All-Government Nanny state. While all who are reading this book know those falsehoods all too well, they bear repeating and highlighting one more time.

What the world and those opposed to us will learn with the creation of the new Republic of Reagan is that secure and sovereign borders *do matter*; faith in God *does matter*; condemning and confronting those who kill "in the name of God" *does matter*; the rule of law *does matter*; keeping the Second Amendment as it is written *does matter*; the facts *do matter*; honest, unbiased education free from the multi-culturism pabulum of the All-Government Nanny state *does matter*; clean, positive, and inspirational entertainment *does matter*; capitalism un-tethered from the social-engineering profit destroying policies of the All-Government Nanny state *does matter*; acceptance to colleges and hiring and promotion based on merit alone *does matter*; holding second-rate and far-left teachers accountable for destroying the futures of our children *does matter*; judges true to the Traditional Values–inspired Constitution of the new nation of Reagan *do matter*; accountability *does matter*; and character *does matter.*

More than that, all of those inside and outside the new nation of Reagan will quickly find that not only do all of those things matter, but they *will* also equal unparalleled success, national solvency, a renewed spirituality, and the highest quality of life on the planet.

The new nation of Reagan will drag the deliberate and highly toxic lies of the far-left and liberal ideology fully into the intense and cleansing rays of the sun and *completely* expose them as the destroyers of faith, families, values, business, truth, profit, education, entertainment, national security, rule of law, and finally, as the destroyers of nations.

If the new nation of Reagan is allowed to peacefully coexist with the corrupt and failing United States of America and the other struggling nations of the world, it will quickly establish itself as *the* model for true peace and prosperity.

It will be the only nation like it on the face of the Earth. The *only* one.

It will be a nation built *entirely* on the *foundation* of Traditional Values.

That eventual reality then creates a new and very interesting dynamic. As the word spreads first from state to state within the United States and then outward across every national border on Earth that the Traditional Values model of government enacted by the Republic of Reagan really *does exist* and is now succeeding like no other and *does prove* the dictates of liberalism, socialism, and the All-Government Nanny state to be a sham and destroyers of virtually all lives and every future, what then happens within the rest of the world?

How would the population of those still living in the failing United States of America react to this obvious and unassailable truth? How would the populations of failing, corrupt, or outright dictatorial nations the world over react?

As far as the rest of the world is concerned and the hundreds of millions of suffering human beings trapped in their very own Hells on Earth, if human nature is any indicator, many of them will also soon beg to join the most successful, solvent, and Traditional Values–driven nation on the planet.

By then, the Republic of Reagan will have undoubtedly grown. By then, at least the states of North Carolina and Alabama would have merged into the only nation on Earth built on our values. These two great states will bring the incalculable treasure of their like-minded people, their land, their industries, their military facilities, and their infrastructures into the confines of our Traditional Values Republic.

Will this now expanded Republic of Reagan accept immigrants from other nations? Eventually. Without a doubt. But *only* if they meet the very strict and *strongly enforced* immigration policies of our new Republic.

For, like the United States of America created by our Founding Fathers, the Republic of Reagan will also be a land of immigrants—a true melting pot filled with one key ingredient: a belief and an allegiance to Traditional Values.

It will be our new nation governed by our beliefs. Period.

With the creation of Reagan, the light of liberty will once again burn bright not only for the hundreds of millions still living in the failed United States of America, but for people the world over to see. Many will naturally be drawn to its warm and comforting glow: a warm, comforting, and liberating light that was envisioned by our advisors and ignited by the millions of Americans willing to step into that arena and scream, "Enough is enough!"

Can *you* imagine it? Can *you* see it? Will *you* be part of it? Will *you* move to it?

As you read these closing words, hundreds of people just like you are *already* working behind the scenes to make it a reality.

They don't think it is a "pipe dream." They *do* believe and they *do* know that, with just 1.5 percent of the population of the current United States of America, this "impossible dream" can be realized.

They believe it *has* to be realized for the honorable reasons that drove them to act.

They will *not* be subservient to the state. They will *not* swallow their pride. They will *never* water down their principles.

They *know* that if we don't make a stand soon, *our values will be swept into the dustbin of history.*

They *do* believe it is noble and right to fight on your feet rather than *exist* on your knees.

They refuse to exist under the dictates of the All-Government Nanny state.

They have no intention of stopping until they are successful.

They have no intention of stopping until they can *finally* hold out their arms to all those willing to embark on this glorious quest and say:

"Welcome to the Republic of Reagan. . . . *Welcome home.*"

INDEX

Huckabee, Mike, 192
Human dignity, 4
Hurlburt Field, 155

Immigration policy, 71–75
"The Impossible Dream" (song), 14
"Is Secession Legal?" (McClanahan),
114–122, 182–183

Jefferson, Thomas, 12, 21, 33,
121–122
The Jewish Daily Forward, 38–39
Jews
September 11th terrorist attack
and, 92–93
during World War II, gun
ownership and, 76–77
Joint Resolution of Secession, 127
Jones, Tommy Lee, 39–40
Judges, 188

Katzenberg, Jeffrey, 36
Kizer, Gene H. Jr., 98, 123–124
Kushner, Tony, 37–38, 40, 41

Labor unions, 80–82
Lee, Robert E., 47–48, 49
Left, the. *See also* Liberals
on Confederate South, 34
courts and, 187–188
creating and protecting the
privileged class, 81
dishonesty of, 174
Disney company/channel and, 65
labeling secessionist movement
members, 192–193
lacking civility and politeness,
57–58

September 11th attack response,
92–93
underestimation of, 186–187
Lenin, Vladimir, 77
Letters from a Farmer in Pennsylvania
(Dickinson), 122
Levin, Mark, 54
Liberals. *See also* Left, the
cable channels and, 24
efforts to disprove God's existence,
24–25
on Founding Fathers, 28
in Hollywood, 93–94
manipulation of history, 36–41
Liberty
growing infringement on, 32
Lord Acton on, 47
Lincoln (film), 37, 38–41
Lincoln, Abraham, 12, 16, 21,
37–46, 49, 50, 98, 118, 126
Lincoln, Mary Todd, 39–40
Livingston, Robert, 33
Longcore, Russel D., 126–132,
132n5
Louisiana, 86–87

MacDill Air Force Base, 155
MacFarlane, Seth, 60, 62–63
MacKinnon, Douglas
hacked devices of, 17–18
meeting with Reagan, 201–207
obstacles overcome during youth,
2–3
option of using a pseudonym, 1–2
Madison, James, 117
"Man in the Arena" speech
(Roosevelt) (1910), 199
Man of La Mancha (play), 14

North Carolina, 160
NRA (National Rifle Association), 76

Obama, Barack, 8, 28, 174
    deity status of, 24
    on Founding Fathers, 28
    global warming and, 79
    "green" agenda of, 145
    gun control and, 76
    hostile to Christian faith, 59–60
    immigration and, 74
    lack of experience, 8
    Levin on Romney's loss to, 54–55
    reaction to reelection of, 85,
        160–161
Obama, Michelle, 65, 66
Obamacare, 66, 82–84
Occupy Wall Street movement,
    173–174
Oil, 144–145
Ordinance of Secession document,
    127, 130–131

Paglia, Camille, 65–66
Patrick Air Force Base, 156
Perry, Katy, 60
Perry, Rick, 161
Pilgrims, 23, 25–27, 169
Political parties, transitioning from
    one corrupt party to another,
    133. See also Democratic Party;
    Republican Party
Proclamation of 1763, 29–30
Pseudonym, used by author, 1–2
Public-employee unions, 80–82

Quartering Act of 1765, 30, 31

Rawle, William, 48–49, 98–113
Reagan, Ronald, 197–207
Red State (website), 68
Referendum, state, 128–129
Religion. See also Christianity/
        Christians
    liberals on, 24–25
    Pilgrims and, 25–26
Republican Party
    immigration policy and, 74, 75
    minority vote and, 72
Republic of Reagan, 209. See also
    New Republic
Revere, Paul, 31, 192
Revolutionary War, 28–32
"The Right of Secession" (Kizer),
    123–124
Right to bear arms, 75–78, 192
Robins Air Force Base, 153
Roosevelt, Teddy, 198–199

Scalia, Antonin, 114, 115
Schlafly, Phyllis, 75
Schmidt, Eric, 174
Science Channel, 24
Science/scientists
    disproving God's existence and, 24
    global warming and, 79
Secession convention, 129–130
Secession from the United States,
    51–88
    Civil War and, 42, 43–44,
        123–124, 125–126
    coming unrest for, 181–189
    first discussions about, 5–8
    growing movement for, 85–88
    justification for dream of, 12–14